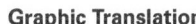

Graphic Translation

A graphic design project guide

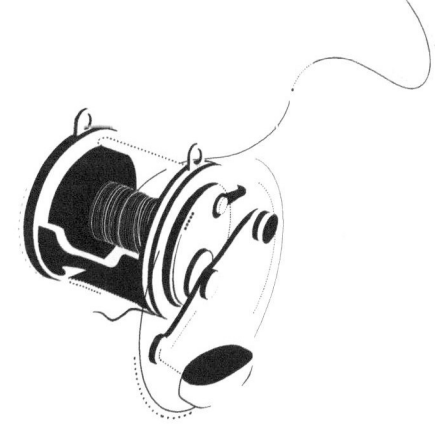

Kimberly Elam

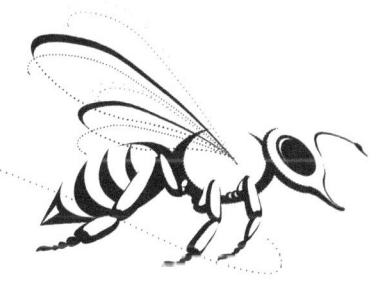

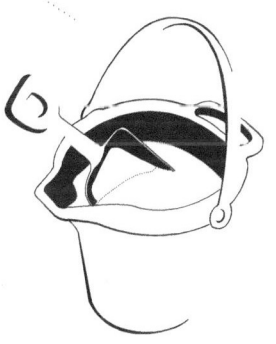

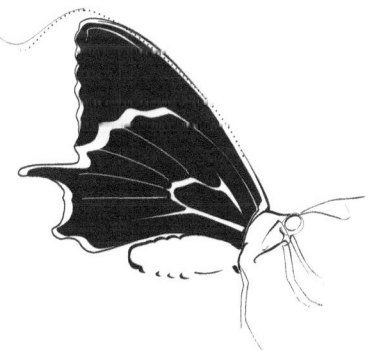

Other Books by Kimberly Elam

Expressive Typography, Van Nostrand Reinhold, 1990

Geometry of Design, Princeton Architectural Press, 2001, papress.com

Grid Systems, Princeton Architectural Press, 2004, papress.com

Typographic Systems, Princeton Architectural Press, 2007, papress.com

Paper Food, ebook, lulu.com

Line Icons, ebook, lulu.com

Additional Titles: Studio**Resource**Inc.com

Elam, Kimberly,
        Graphic translation / Kimberly Elam.
ISBN: 1-4196-5332-6

To order additional copies, contact:
BookSurge.com
1-866-308-6235
orders@booksurge.com

Book & Cover Design
Kimberly Elam

Cover Illustration
Ronnie Koff

Graphic Translation

Table of Contents

Introduction

Graphic translation produces drawings of instant recognition and startling visual interest. The work in this book focuses on iconic representation, which is a simplified version of the object, with the visual essence of the object retained. Graphic translation is as much art as it is design. The examples portray a multitude of individual approaches to the drawing system and give the designer, educator, and student insight into learning this method of graphic drawing.

All of the drawings were accomplished in my basic design courses at the Ringling School of Art and Design. Digital media is ideal for this drawing process and Adobe Illustrator software was used in all of the drawings. Through computer drawing the designer can approach the project with scanned images as visual templates for drawing reference, and collage images in order to create the best image reference possible. The computer enables a visual record to be made of all phases of drawing without fear losing or destroying earlier versions.

I was first introduced to the process of graphic translation at a summer graphic design workshop in Brissago, Switzerland, sponsored by Kent State University. At that workshop a drawing master from the Schule für Gestaltung in Basel, Kurt Hauert, conducted a project in graphic translation of nature and water. At first I was skeptical as to how green leaves and the constantly changing tones of lake water could be drawn in black and white. Students worked with plaka, a dense opaque white and black paint, first on paper and later painting on glass placed over the paper. The resulting drawings were startlingly crisp organic forms with light and dark highlights and reflections on foliage and waves. These drawings remain in my mind today.

The intent of this book and others in the series is to thank my students for all they have taught me and to share with others approaches and methodology that may prove useful. Design education is a fluid process that constantly evolves. Designers and design educators are invited to share the results of their experiences with me for inclusion in later printings of this work.

Kimberly Elam

Choosing the Pose or Point of View

The process of graphic translation is complex and is best accomplished as a series of steps. The first of these steps is to produce a drawing of the object, and in order to do this the designer needs reference for the drawing such as the object itself, or a detailed drawing, and/or a series of detailed photographs. When collecting reference for drawing it is important to select a view of the object that is descriptive in silhouette. If the object is readily identifiable in silhouette it is likely that the translation drawing series will produce a series of readily understandable drawings.

For example, if the object chosen for graphic translation is an elephant, a front view of the elephant would not work well as in silhouette it appears to be a non-descriptive blocky creature. The visual essence of the elephant is in the identification of the trunk, tusks, triangular ears, and square torso with a small wispy tail. A side view would work much better as in silhouette it would be readily recognized as an elephant and most of the key features would be apparent. Better still a side view that has the trunk in an interesting curvilinear position would yield a yet more recognizable elephant.

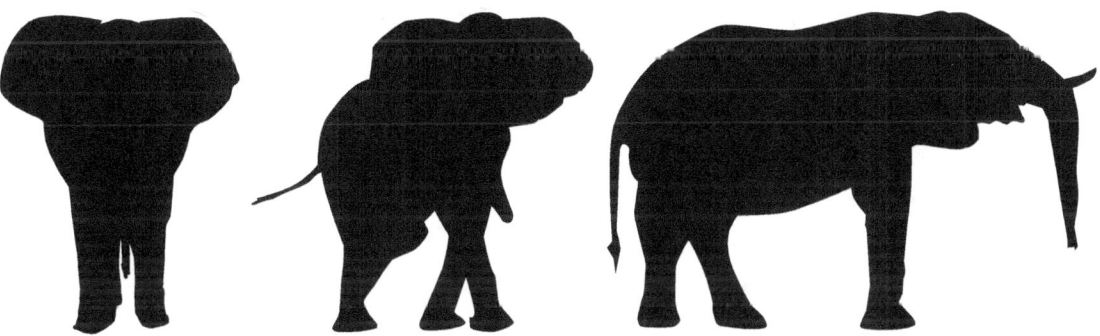

Front View
A front view (left) will be prob-
lematic because it will result in
a silhouette that is difficult to
readily recognize as an elephant
at a glance. Since the trunk and
profile are important in visual
identification further research is
needed with alternate views.

Three-Quarters View
A three-quarters view (middle) is
better but the position of the legs
is awkward.

Side View
The side profile view of the
elephant is better because the
identifiable visual clues will be
present in the silhouette: trunk,
tusks, tail, and torso. In profile,
the drawing will be unmistakably
an elephant.

Gathering Reference Images & Copyright

Copyright infringement issues occur with photographic reference because a drawing from a photographic template is considered a derivative work. This means that if a photograph is downloaded from the internet or scanned from a book to be used as drawing reference, that permission and/or a fee for use is due to the copyright holder.

Working with your own photographs or copyright free images avoids this problem. The elephant images below are just a few available from Dover Publications. Doverpublications.com, publishes hundreds of royalty free, excellent quality, clip art image books and their entire collection can be bought on CD. Some photographic image CDs are also copyright free and are usually advertised as such. When working with images from professional resources, such as internet image banks, a fee must be paid in order to download and use the image as reference for the drawing.

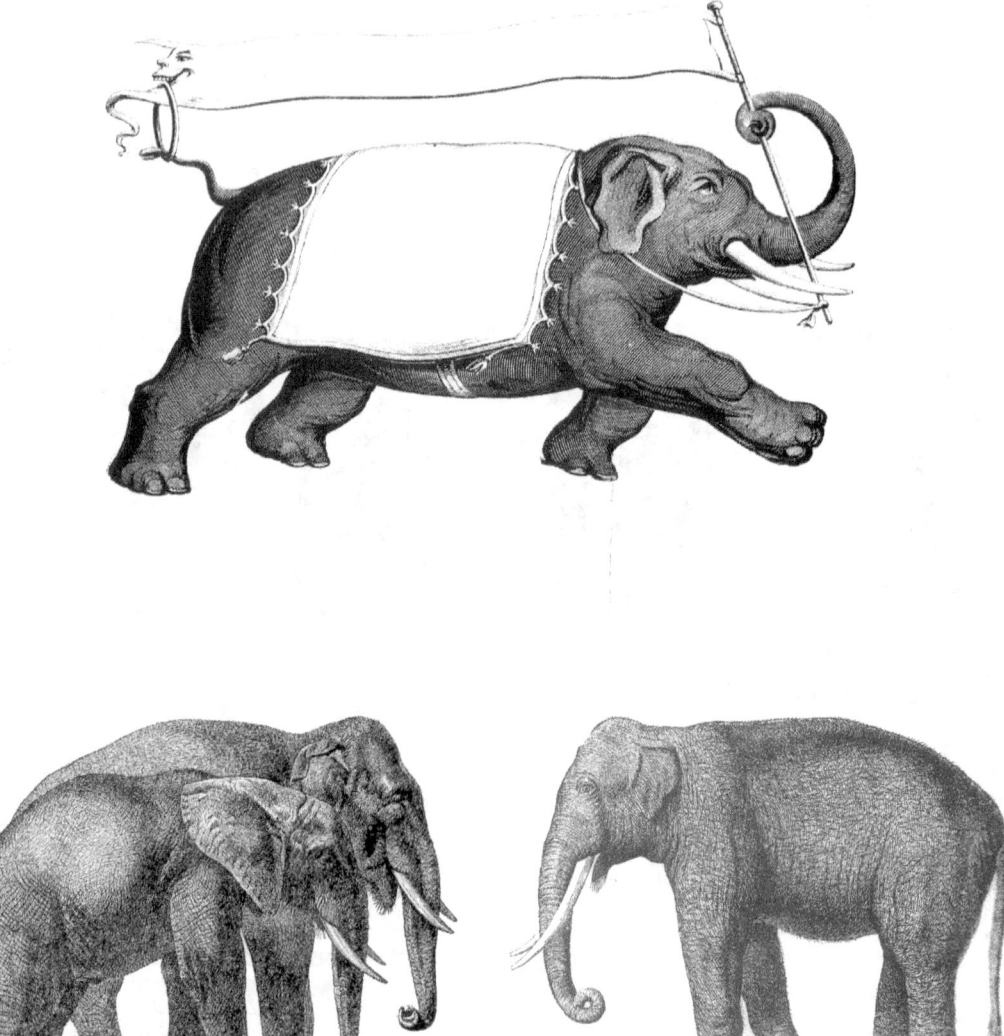

Using a Template

Scanned reference is imported into a vector drawing software. All of the images in this book were drawn with Adobe Illustrator. Lock the reference in place and draw on top of it with a brightly colored line so that it can easily be seen against the grayscale reference. Working in layers is recommended so that the reference can be "locked" and the drawing periodically checked for accuracy.

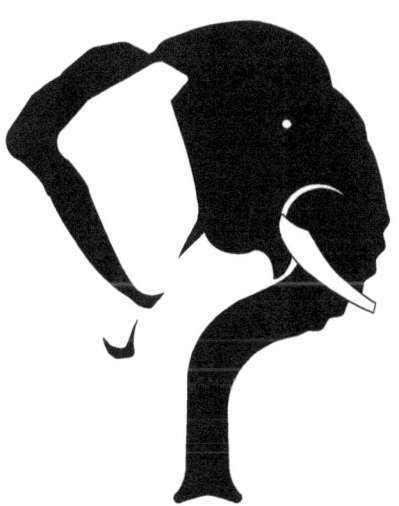

Templates
The two posters (below) are Russian zoo posters from the 1920s. The stylized reference of an elephant assist the designer in drawing, stylizing, and detailing the elephant's head. The posters were scanned and used as a template for drawing.

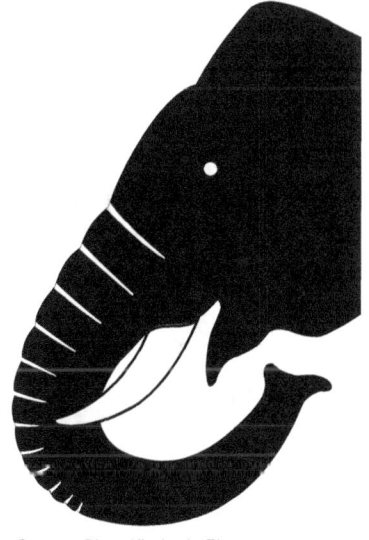

Syreeta Pitts, Kimberly Elam

Dimitri Bulanov,, 1927
Zoo Poster, left

Dimitri Bulanov, 1928
Zoo Poster, Right

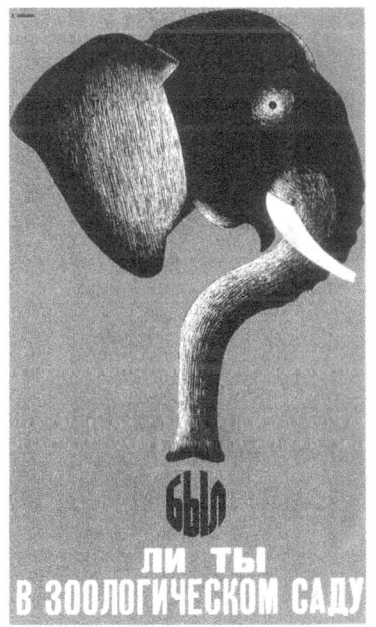

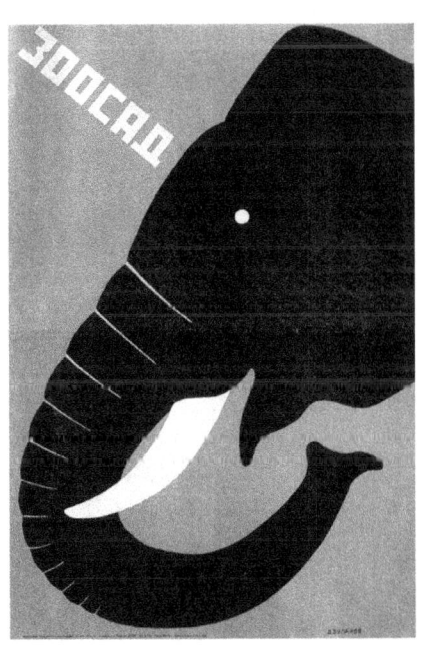

Translation Steps

The most important step in the process of graphic translation is the first step, which is creating the original drawing. This drawing should be a stylized representational drawing with enough detail to work with throughout the process. It is of utmost importance that ever part of the drawing be drawn on the computer with closed paths. Closed paths can be stroked or filled at will without juggling objects that are in front of or behind others.

Once a strong first drawing is created the designer is able to focus on the graphic translation steps one at a time. A good first step is to experiment with shade and shadow. This process gives the illusion of a light source and often makes the object feel more three dimensional. Working with the shade and shadow drawings, the designer can begin looking for opportunities to create closure by selectively eliminating lines. This part of the process makes the

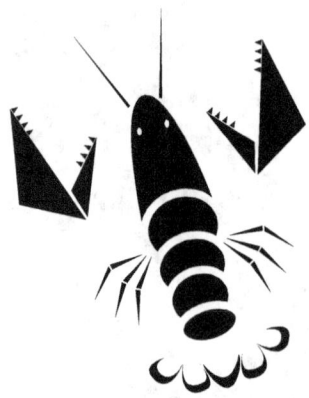

Filled Original Drawing
All portions of the object are
drawn as closed paths.

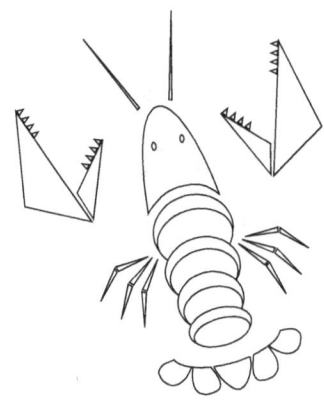

Line Original Drawing
All portions of the object are
drawn as closed paths.

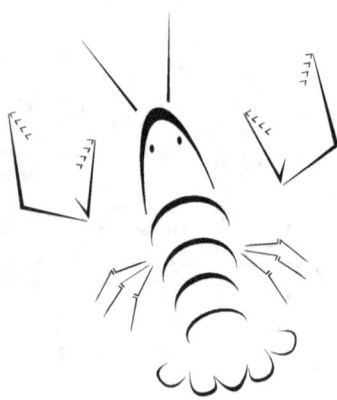

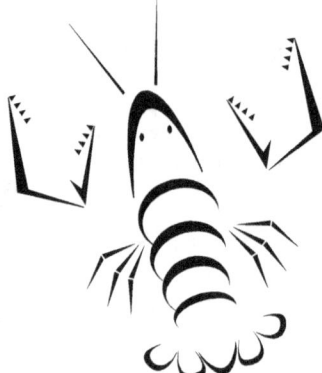

Experiments with Shade and
Shadow

This is the inverse of the drawing to the left.

Translation Steps

object visually interesting as the viewer's mind completes the missing lines. The final step is to look for opportunities to convert lines to points with dotted lines. This effect is subtle and rhythmically guides the viewer's eye.

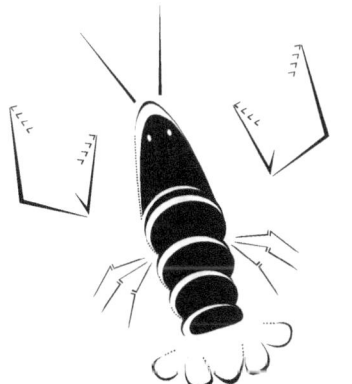
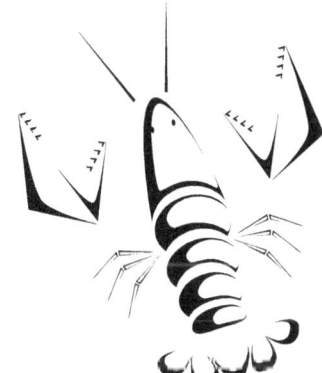
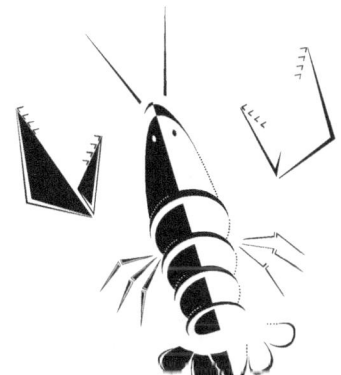

Experiments with Shade and
Shadow

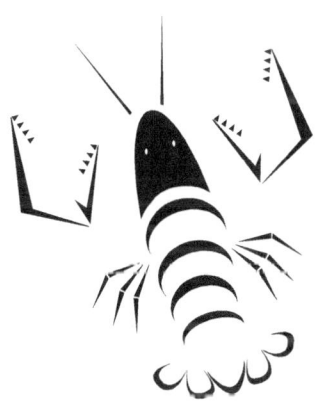
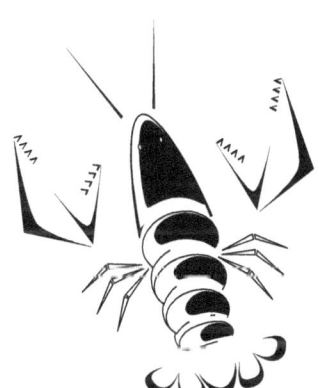
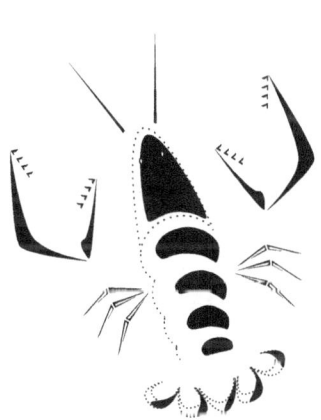

Experiments with Closure

Converting Lines to Points

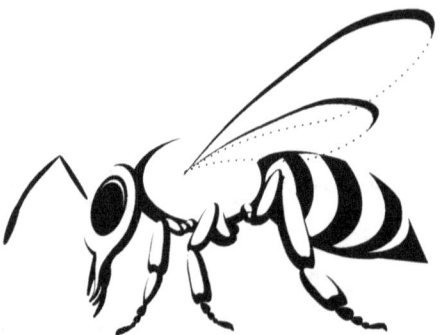

Original drawing and starting point for Loni Diep.

Loni Diep's Process

Most students begin the process of graphic translation from a representational drawing that is simplified and through a series of steps becomes more complex with experiments in shade and shadow and point and line. Loni Diep, however, immediately understood the process and produced the drawing, left, as the first step. Her process is unusual in that from the first drawing she worked backward to refine and detail her work. Her process is followed on the next four pages with her comments.

"This is the image I originally started out with. So I had to work backwards in the translation, which seemed pointless at first. But it helped me see flaws in individual components of the drawing. Also, it helped by producing elements in the beginning simple steps that worked with later final steps."

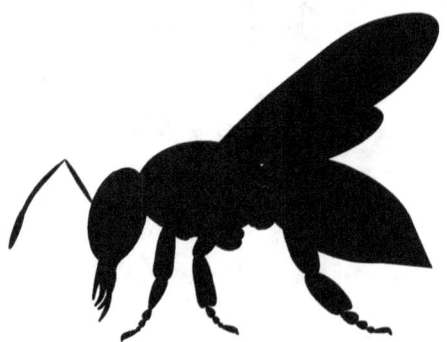

1. Silhouette

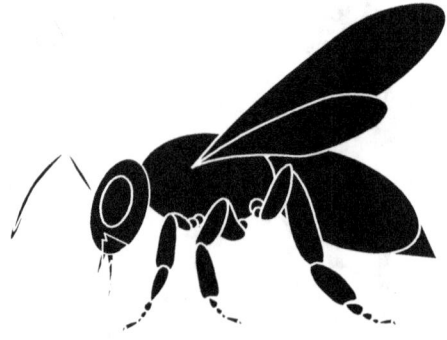

2. Outline
"When the mouth is outlined, a lot of the details disappear. I thought the mouth looked better simple so in the final steps the mouth was simplified to one part."

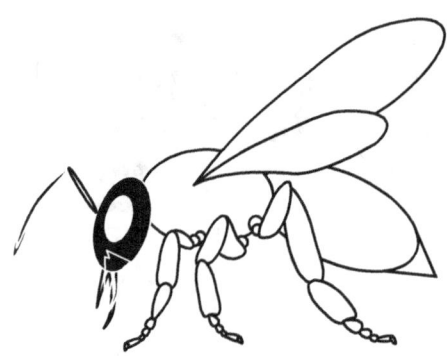

3. Inverse of Step 2

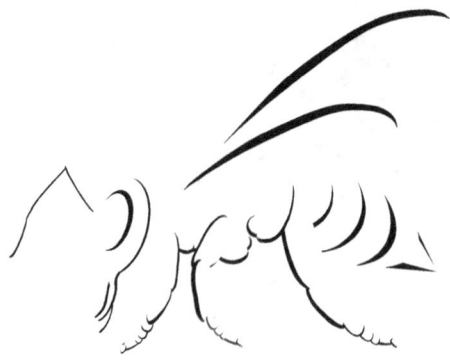

4. Closure
"I defined planes with hints of shadows."

6

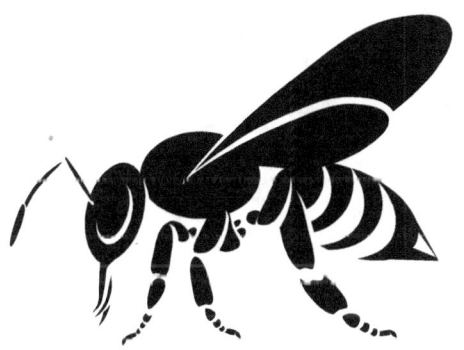

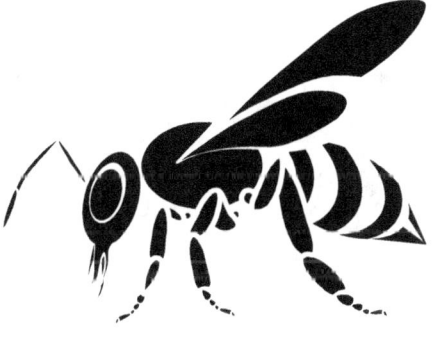

5. Inverse of step 4.
"I moved the black forms so that the white shadows are more dramatic."

6. Adjustment
"I moved around and re-sized black shapes from step 5 and outlined legs in white. I was just experimenting with the forms just to see what it would look like."

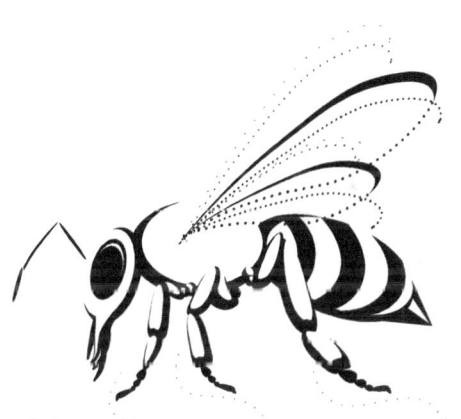

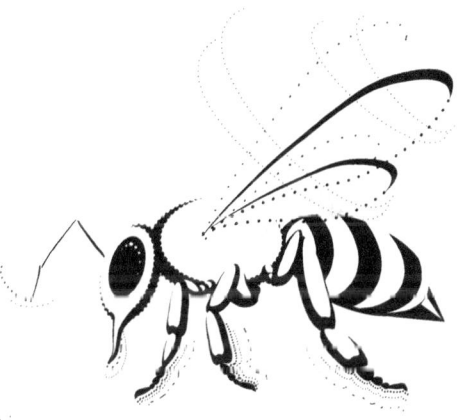

7. Refinement
Refined version of step 6

8. Mouth
"I simplified mouth because of results from step 2."

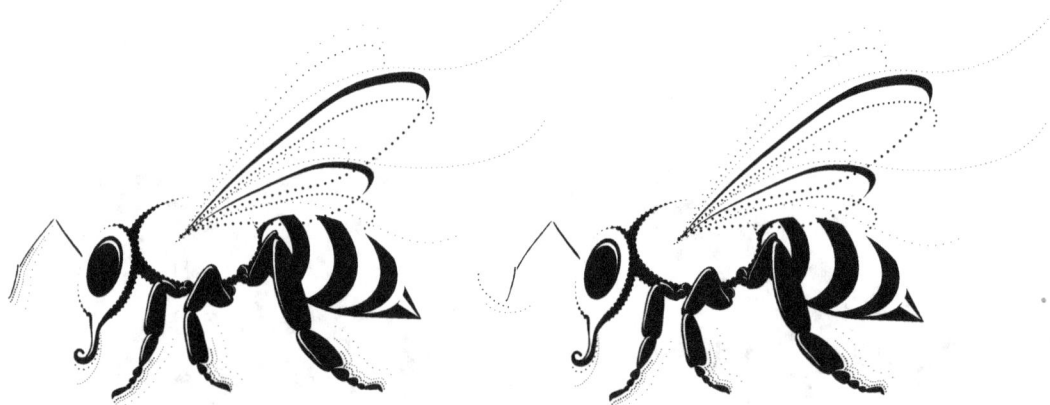

9. Wings
"I mixed wings from step 8 with motion lines."

10. Antenna
"I changed lines on the antenna."

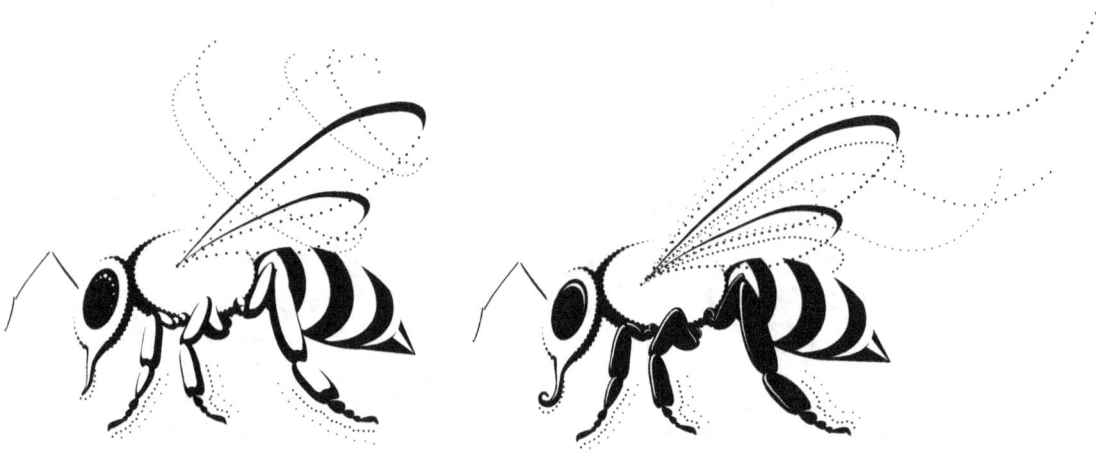

11. Lines as Points
"I copied and pasted step 10 and simplified some of the dotted lines around the legs and antenna, and also made the dotted lines a little heavier, so that they are easier to read."

12. Motion Lines
"I copied and pasted step 11 and tried to fix motion lines on the wings to give it more movement, and also simplified dotted lines around antenna, eye, and legs."

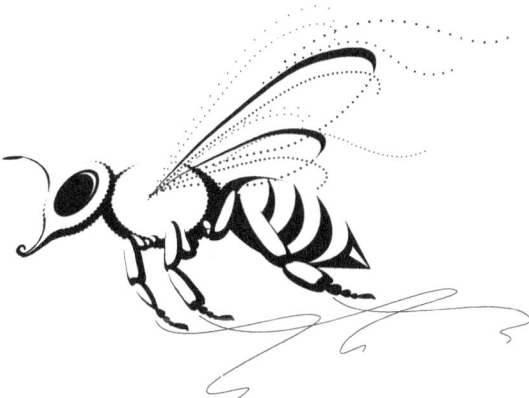

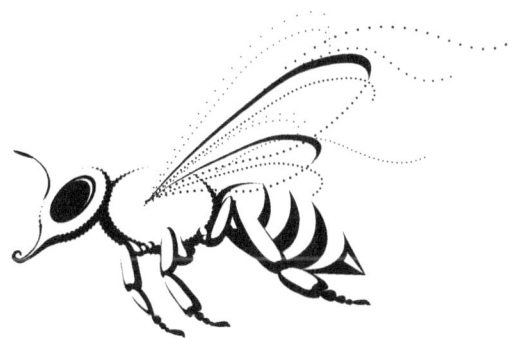

13. Motion Lines

"I tried to fix the motion lines on the legs, since the dotted lines from previous steps crowded the image, and tried to fix the antenna so it would not look like the bee flew into a wall. I adjusted the weight and position of lines in the wings. Angled legs backward to give a sense of motion."

14. Adjustment

"I didn't like the lines on the legs from step 16, so I deleted them."

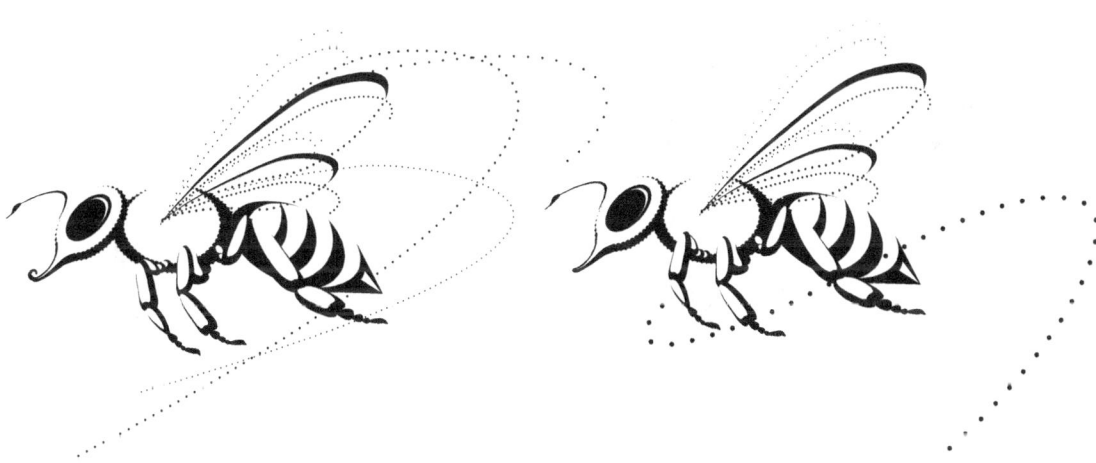

15. Refinement

"The wispy lines on the wings in step 16 and 17 looked awkward and didn't have enough motion, so I adjusted them to give them more speed, and adjusted the antenna to echo the curves in the wing and emphasis the forward motion."

16. Refinement

"I thought there were too many dotted lines in the wings in step 18, so moved motion lines from wings to legs. A heavy dotted line by legs emphasizes the motion of the entire bee."

Drawing With Closed Paths, Copy & Rotate

Objects that are symmetrical can often be drawn most efficiently by drawing half of the object and then copying and reflecting the drawn half to complete the object. The two halves will need to be joined or merged but the process results in perfect symmetry.

Objects that have a multiple of similar parts, such as the fan blades below, can most efficiently be drawn using a copy and repeat process. One of the parts is drawn, selected, and moved or rotated. The result is that there is continuity in the drawing.

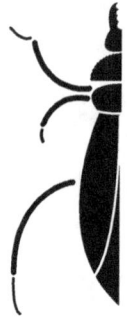

1. Symmetrical Objects
For all symmetrical object draw one half of the object.

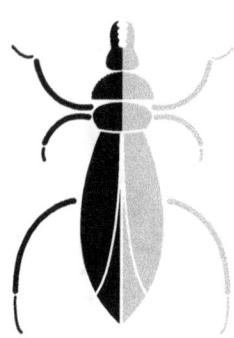

2. Symmetrical Objects
Select and reflect the drawn half of the object.

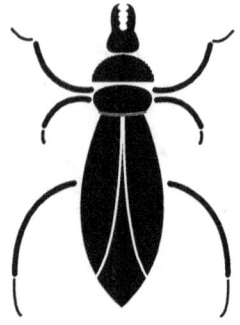

3. Symmetrical Objects
Join the halves of the object to create a completely symmetrical object.

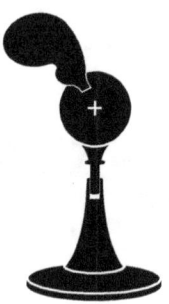

1. Repetitive Objects
When drawing objects that have repetitive parts, such as the fan blades, draw one blade.

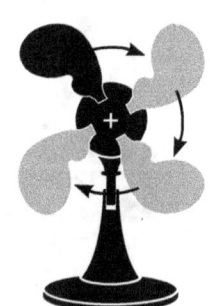

2. Repetitive Objects
Select the blade and copy and rotate from a center point.

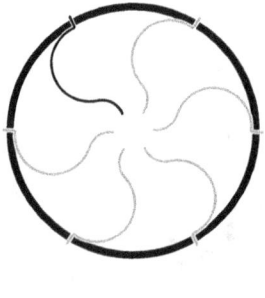

3. Repetitive Objects
The same process is used for the curves of the blade guard cage. Draw one guard and copy and rotate from a center point.

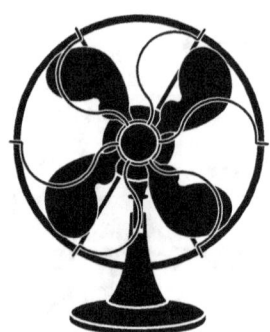

Final Fan Drawing

Creating Shade and Shadow

Each individual surface of the object must be drawn as a closed path that can be individually filled or stroked later. Shapes should be simplified yet retain interesting details that will yield visual interest in the finished drawing. Care should be taken with the portions of the object that com-municate its visual essence. Once the object is drawn with closed paths individual portions of the object can be copied, filled with white, and pasted on top of the original drawing. This process enables the designer to create the illusion of a light source as well as create a light source.

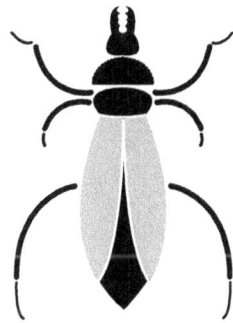 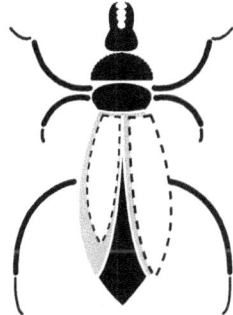 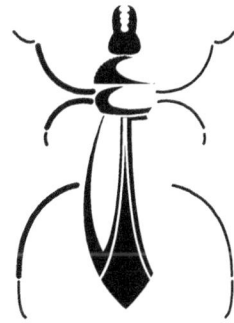 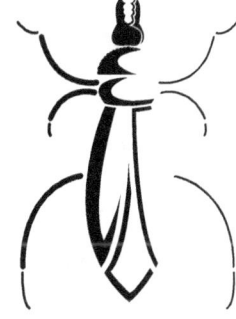

1. Shade & Shadow
To create the illusion of shade and shadow select a portion of the object and then copy and place in front.

2. Shade & Shadow
Resize the pasted portions of the object and fill with white.

3. Shade & Shadow
Adjust the position of the pasted white portions to create the illu-sion of a light source.

4. Shade & Shadow
Repeat the process with other portions of the object to com-plete the illusion.

Creating Shade and Shadow

After the object has been drawn in black and white with appropriate areas filled, a first step is to determine a light source and create shadow. Shadows are often stylized to mimic the forms of the object and add visual interest, such as the curvilinear shadows on the roach. Symmetrical objects often benefit from being split into positive and negative halves, such as the dragonfly. The hard geometric forms of the juicer and sand pail lend themselves to hard geometric shadows which create an elegant play of dark and light.

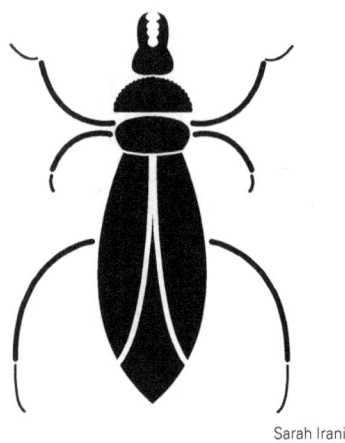

Sarah Irani

Original beetle drawing

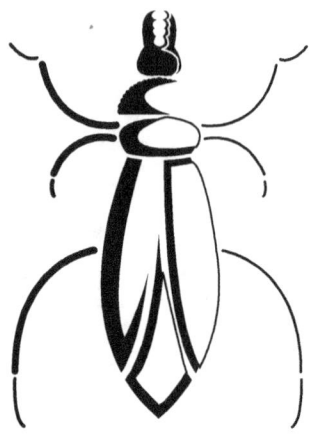

Beetle drawing with shade and shadow

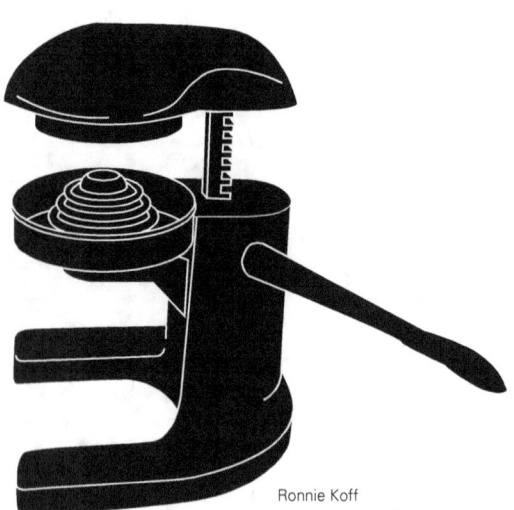

Ronnie Koff

Original juicer drawing

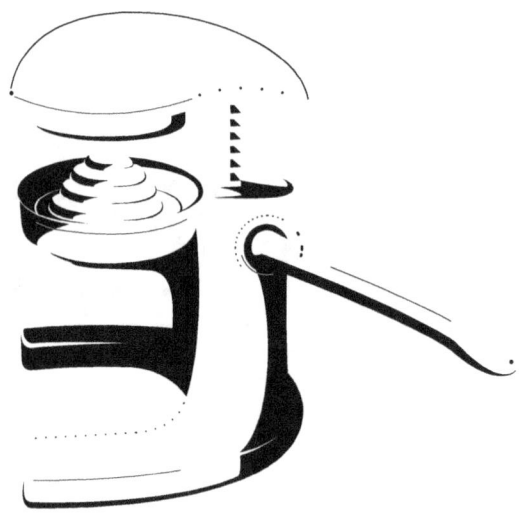

Juicer drawing with shade and shadow

Creating Shade and Shadow

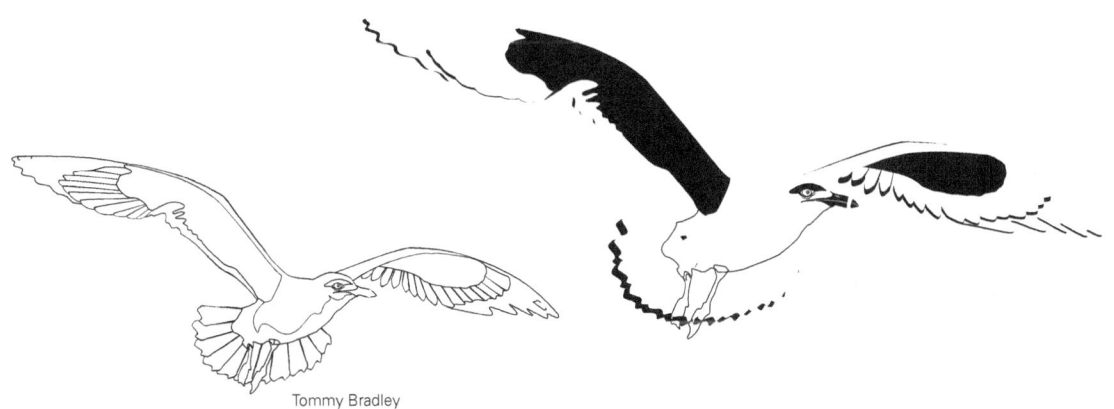

Tommy Bradley

Original seagull drawing

Seagull drawing with shade and shadow

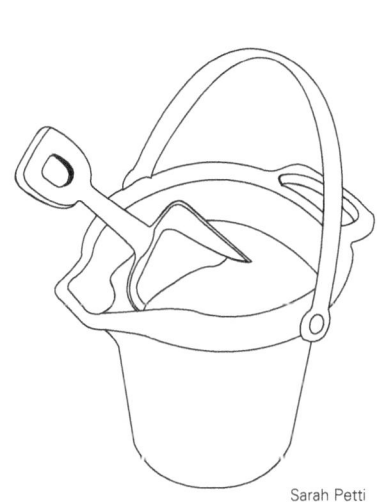

Sarah Petti

Original sand pail drawing

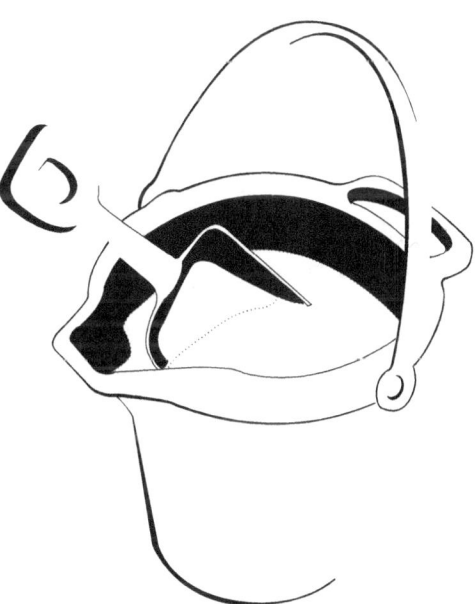

Sand pail drawing with shade and shadow

Silhouette Test

A quick drawing of the image in silhouette will test the pose of the object or creature. If the object or creature is readily identifiable in silhouette it will more than likely work well in the process of graphic translation. The silhouette should reveal the "essence" of the object or creature. The "essence" are those physical aspects that are uniquely identifiable to the subject.

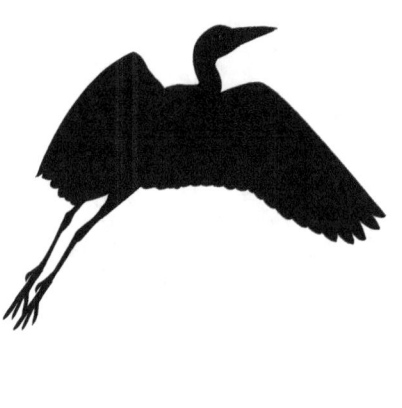
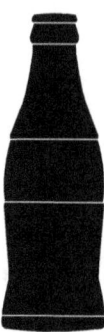
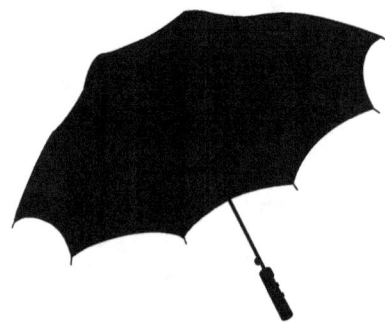

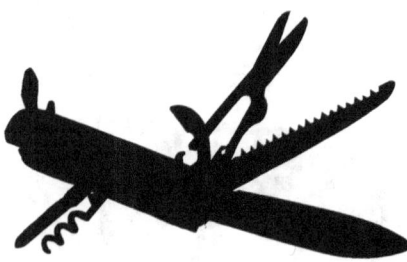

Visual Punctuation

The technique of line and dot is very effective in guiding the viewer's eye. The eye moves along the line and then stops and rests at the dot. This can be seen on the top and left middle surface of the motor, and becomes visual punctuation.

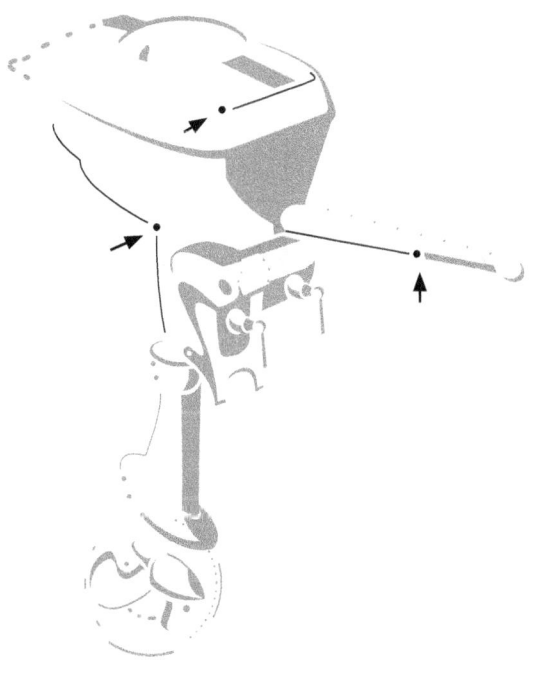

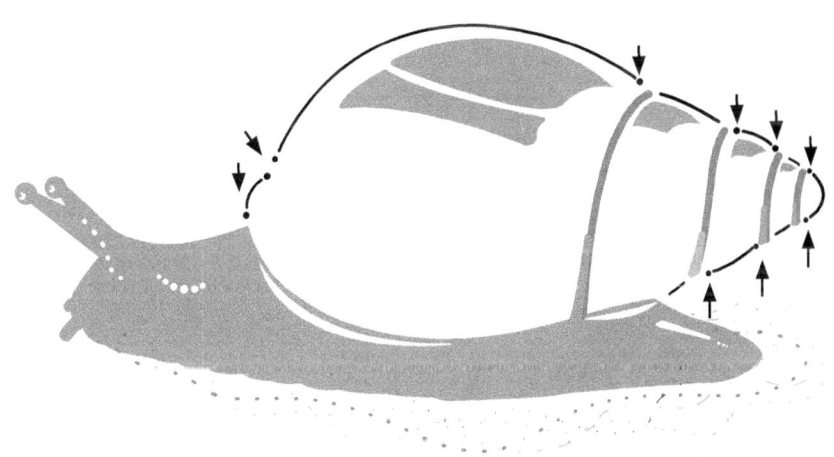

Drawing Eyes

Eyes will always be a point of visual interest and focus for a graphic translation of any creature. Stylization of the eye is an important step in creating a compelling translation. Because there is almost always a circle as the pupil the viewer will be drawn to this element of the drawing first. The goal in drawing the eye is not to recreate reality but to simplify and convincingly portray the eye. Because eyes are a point of focus they should be slightly enlarged to enhance the visual interest.

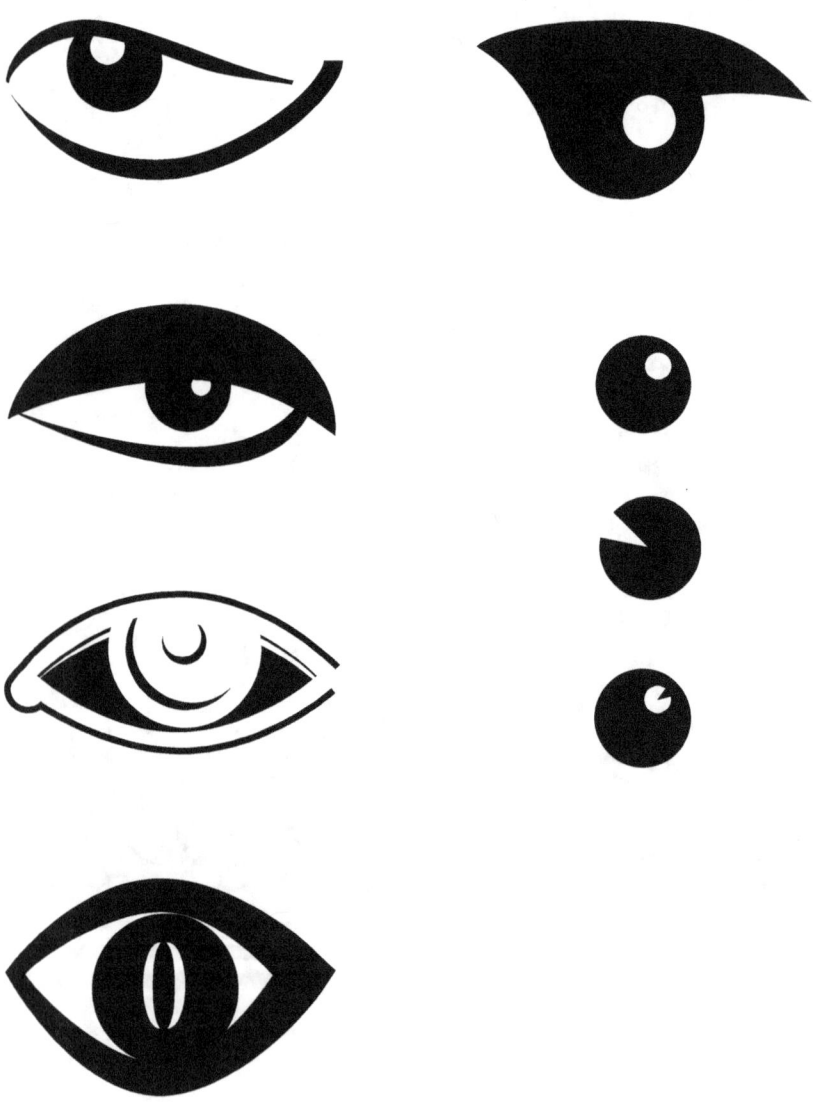

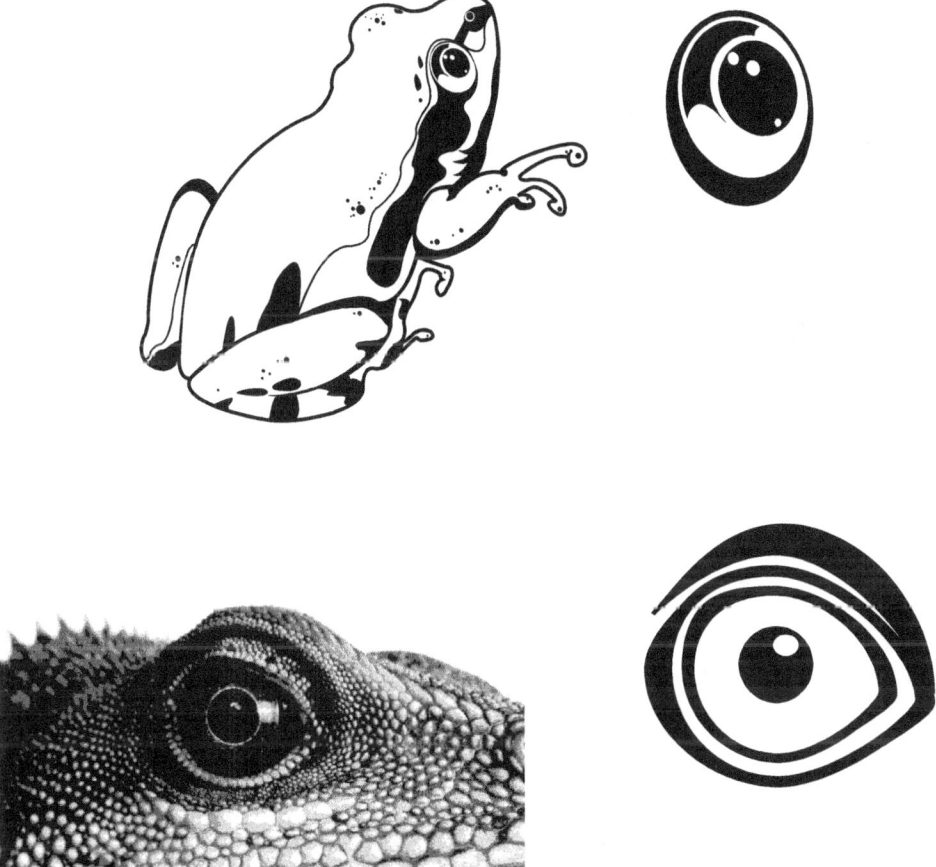

Repetition

Many objects from both the natural and man-made environments have areas of repetition that can become points of visual engagement in a drawing. Often it is possible to stylize and simplify these textures in order to add visual interest. Computer drawing makes repetition a fairly simple process by permitting the shape or texture to be drawn once and then copied and pasted. The segments on the tail of the lobster offer an opportunity for repetition which give a sense of continuity to the drawing as does the texture on the alligator's back. A single fan blade can be drawn once and then copied and rotated to create the other three blades. The lines that are the ridges on the shell can be drawn once and then rotated/copied to create the shell. In all of the drawings repetition and texture serves to move the viewers eye along and around the figure.

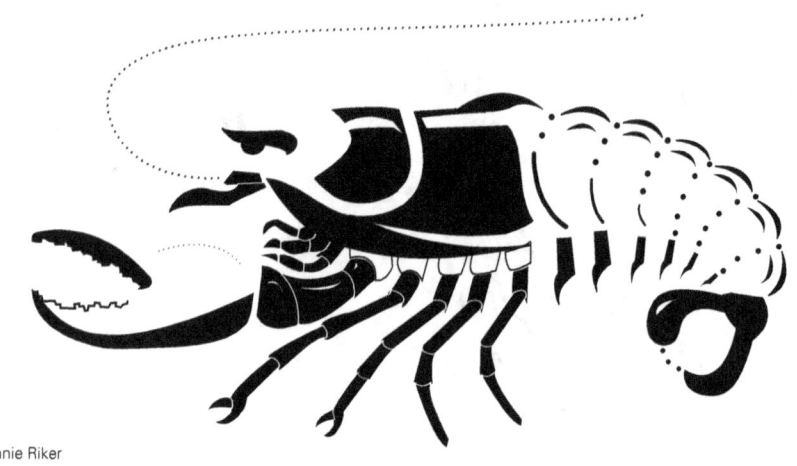

Annie Riker

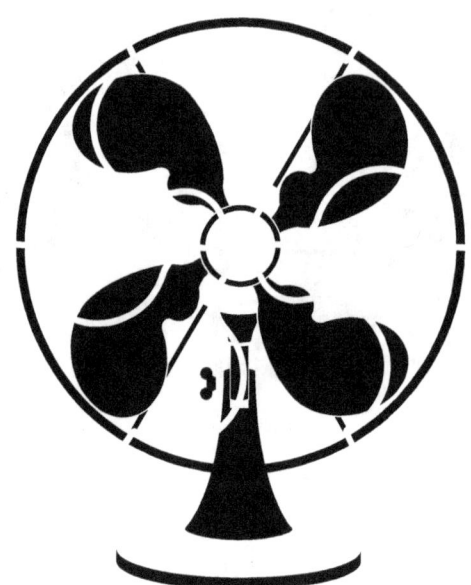

Brian Mah

Repetition

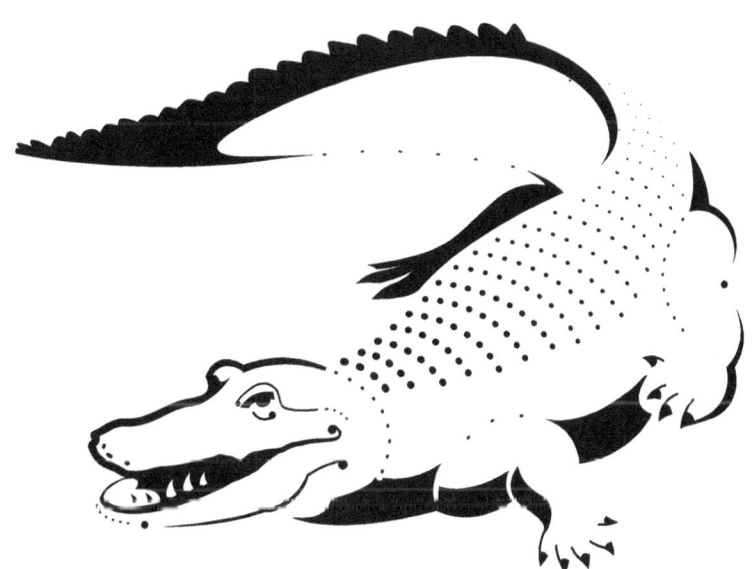

Ronnie Koff

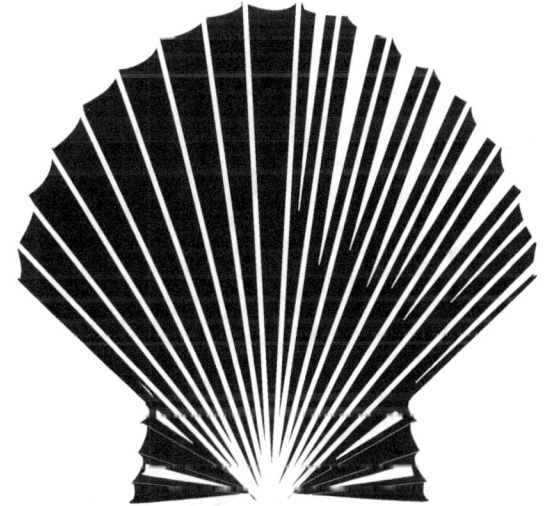

Amy Leet

Closure

The visual principle of closure is that the human eye will complete a figure with incomplete visual information as clues. Once the drawing begins to develop through the graphic translation process it becomes possible to employ closure by selectively deleting portions of lines. This process not only makes the object more interesting but also allows the background white space to become a part of the drawing. With many objects the principle of closure can be pushed to eliminate a remarkable amount of visual information.

The forms of the roach seem to fade as if from a bright light source. The missing lines allow the white of the background to move into the figure and add visual interest as the shapes are completed in the viewer's mind. The lobster below becomes almost unrecognizable as lines are stripped away. In all three drawings the principle of closure makes the result far more visually engaging.

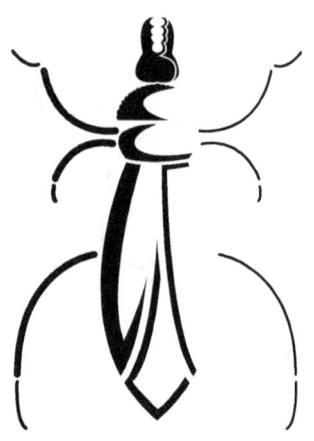

Sarah Irani

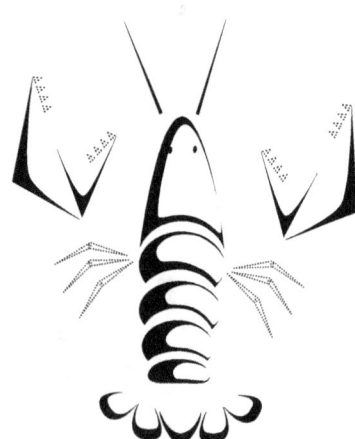

Keishea Edwards

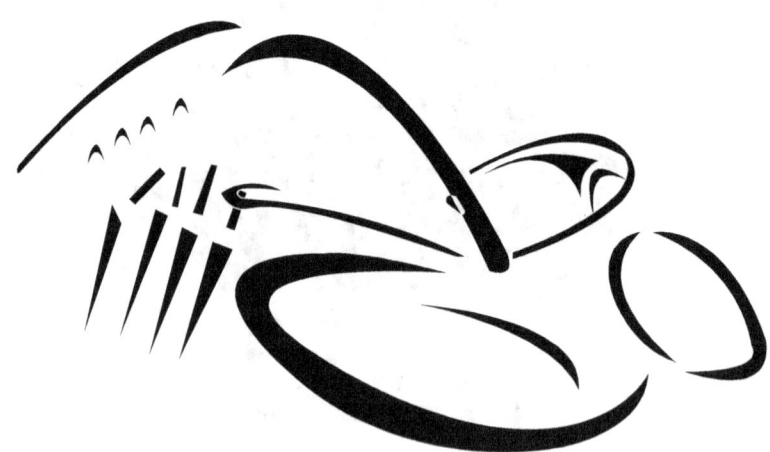

Geoff Pawlaczyk

Converting Lines to Points

Points, lines, and planes are the basic visual elements. As the translation process progresses it becomes possible to convert lines to a series of points. This enhances closure of the line and provides visual clues for closure, the imagined completion of the line. The dotted line is ambiguous in the way it divides space; it is there and not there. The dotted line may be regular in pattern or possibly a rhythmical pattern moving from small dots to larger ones. The rhythm of the dots guides the eye and contrasts with solid lines and filled plane areas.

The lines in the flower, umbrella, and sandal provide contrast to the solid forms and are visual hints of closure. The change in the size of dots in the heel of the sandal move the viewer's eye around the form. The shadowed dots on the right side of the flower are particularly elegant.

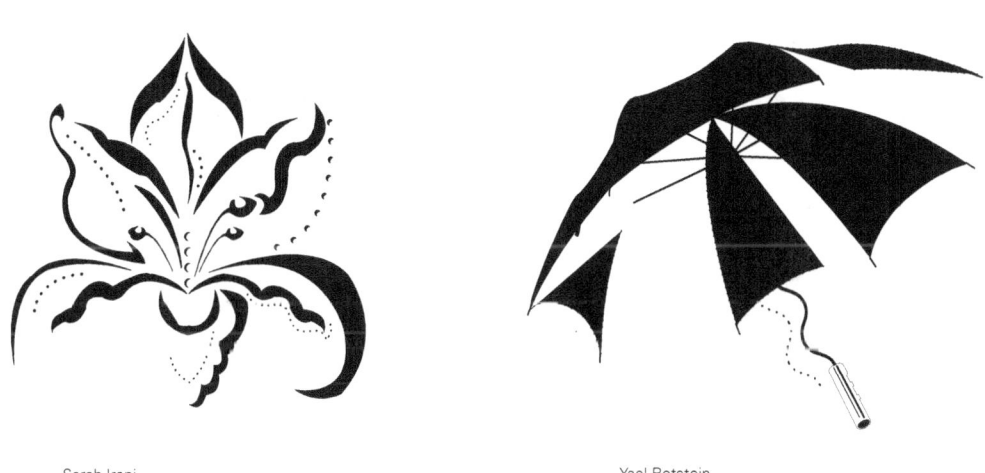

Sarah Irani

Yael Rotstein

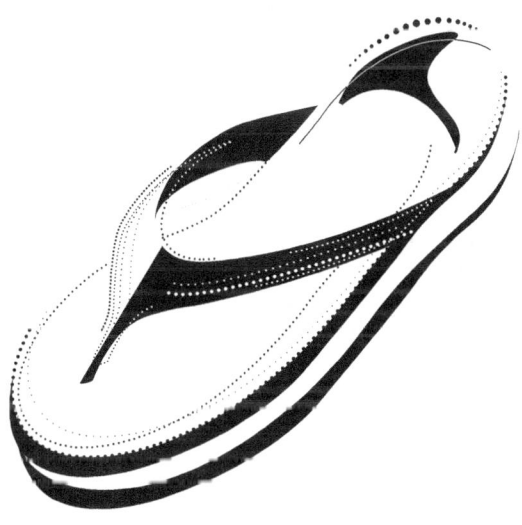

Elaine Fong

Communicating Movement

A final step of transformation for many objects is to communicate movement or function through drawing. Since this communication is done on a static surface, the use of repetition and dotted lines are often used to give the illusion of movement. The dotted line is special because it is ambiguous in space as the background flows through and around it; it is there and not there. This ambiguity makes it an ideal representation of something that moves, such as fluttering wings – they are there and not there.

The initial pose of the bee was static and at rest (left). In order to make the bee more dynamic the position of the head was rotated up and legs were rotated back (right) so that it appeared to be in flight. Repetition of dotted lines of varying weight were used to make the wings appear to flutter and the thin solid lines near the legs portray the smooth irregular motion of a bee. The ladybug as well initially appeared at rest. The use of rhythmical repetition of the wings gives the illusion of movement.

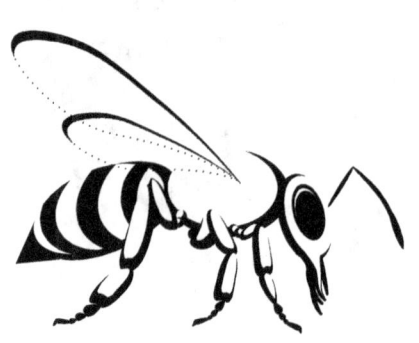

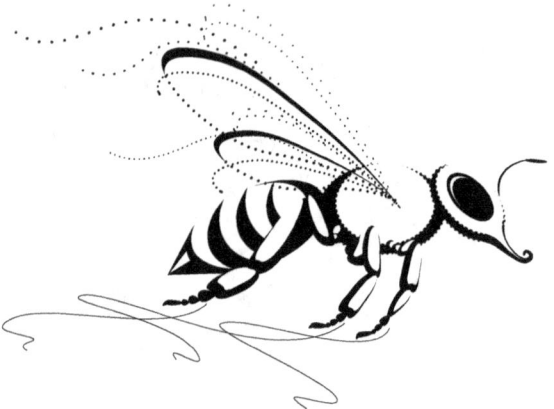

Loni Diep

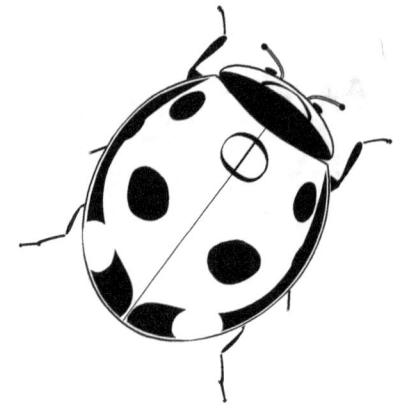

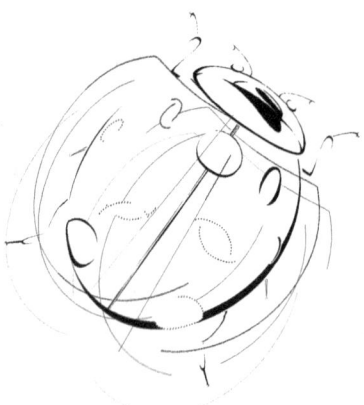

Heather Hickman

Communicating Movement

The Egret wings already appear to be moving in the original drawing pose. The addition of repeated dotted lines enhances the illusion of movement as does the new position of the legs rotated and swept backwards. Arcs of lines enhance the illusion of flapping wings.

Some creatures, because of a static pose, do not easily lend themselves to the idea of movement. The frog is given a sense of movement with the addition of a tongue that is capturing an insect, and the snail can appear to be crawling up a wall through rotation.

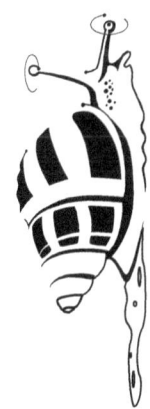

Chris Roeleveld

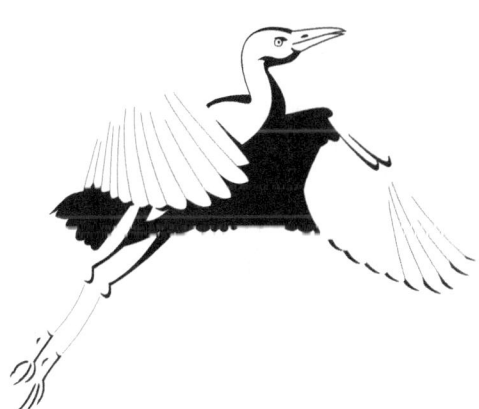

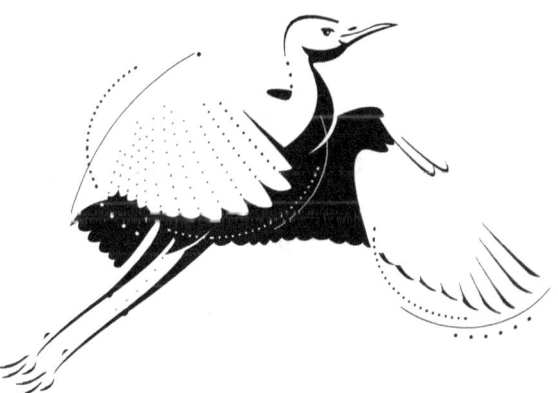

Ronnie Koff

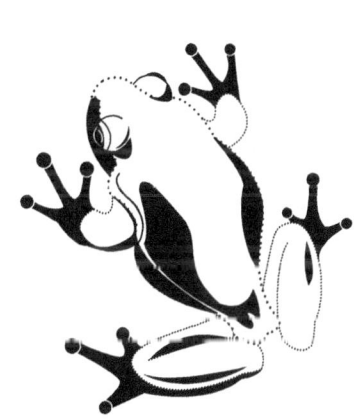

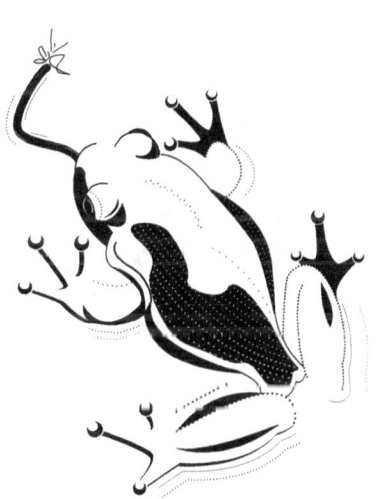

Jeremy Kennedy

23

Communicating Function

Man-made objects can also be given a sense of "life" by the communication of movement through their function. The addition of the illusion of movement heightens visual interest as the mind replays the sight and sound of these common functions, such as the whir of line as it leaves the reel or the hum of the blender as it mixes liquid. Since the diagonal is the most active and unstable visual direction the ceiling fan, blender, and guitar are all rotated diagonally.

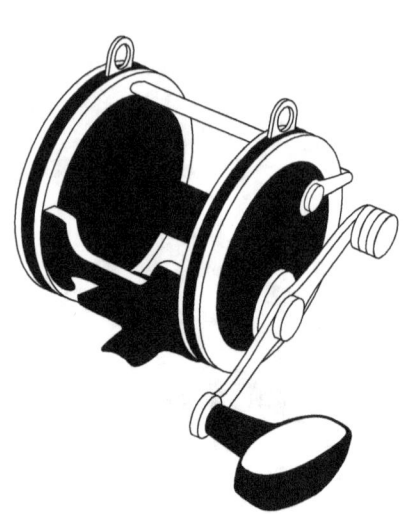

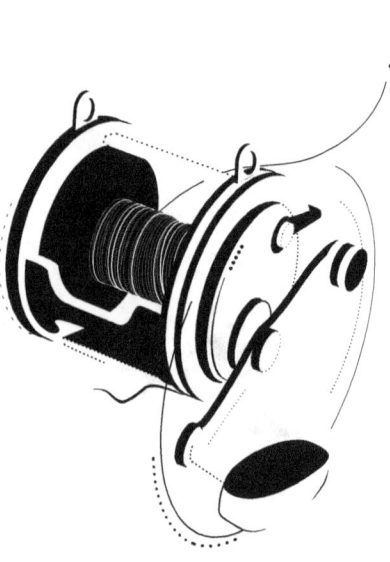

Jason Richardson

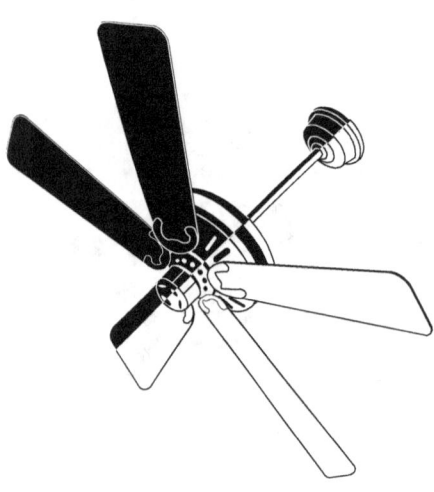

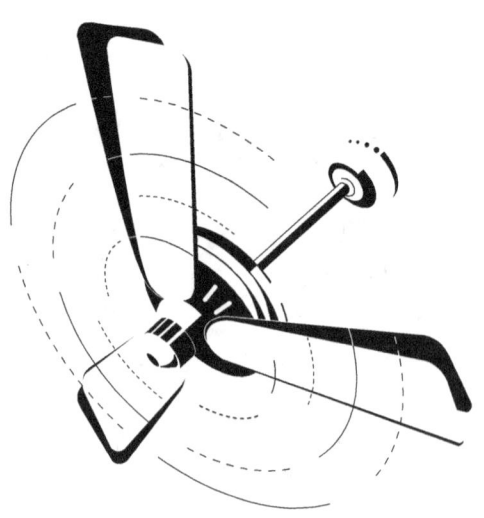

Jeremy Kennedy

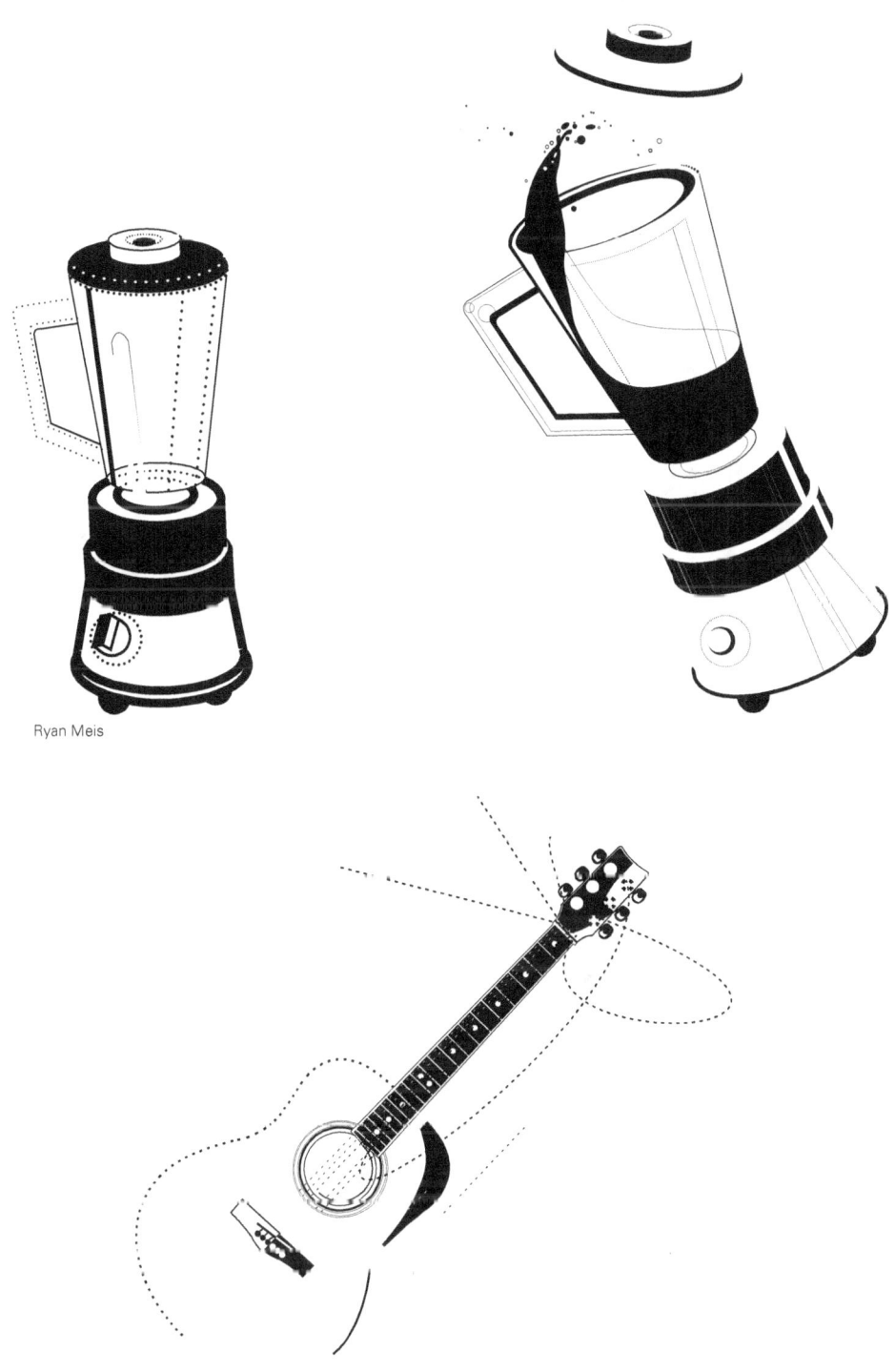

Ryan Meis

Glen Bowman II

Style

Graphic translation is a system of drawing but it is by no means a formula that produces similar results. The process is as much art as design and unique individual style always comes into play. There are four different lobster drawings each done by a different designer. While the subject is the same, each of the drawings is distinctly individual. Lobster 1 uses a top view pose and highly abstracted geometric forms. Lobster 2 and lobster 3 used exactly the same draw-

ing reference and pose, yet the drawings are unique in style and approach. Lobster 4 is the most highly abstracted with geometric forms and a strong reliance on closure.

A similar situation exists in the translations of umbrellas. Each designer has chosen reference and worked with that reference to develop a drawing with a play of light as shade and shadow.

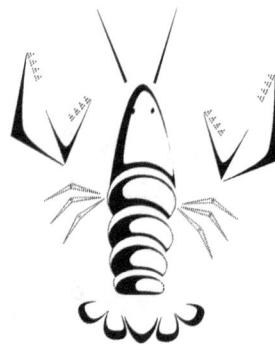

Lobster 1
Keishea Edwards

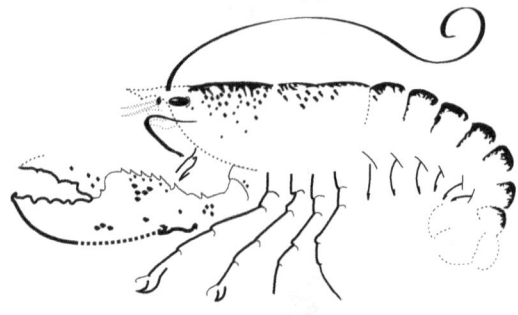

Lobster 2
Jana Dee Bassingthwaite

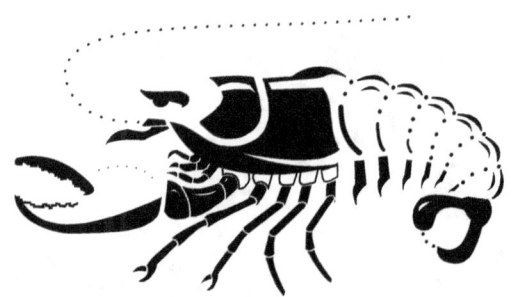

Lobster 3
Annie Riker

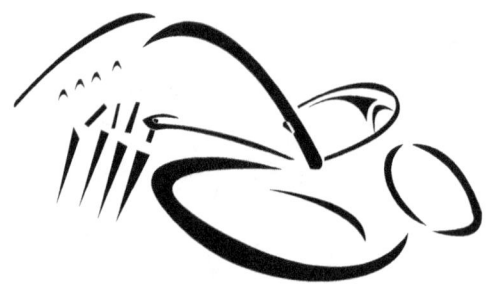

Lobster 4
Geoff Pawlaczyk

Style

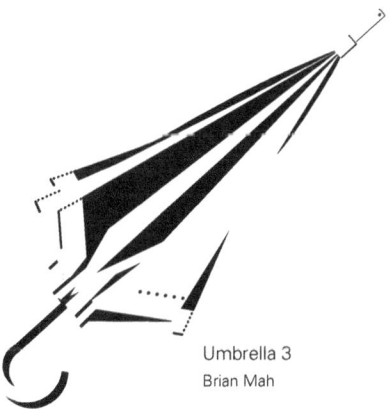

Umbrella 3
Brian Mah

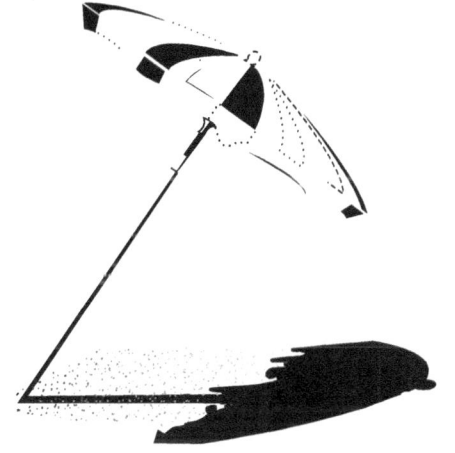

Umbrella
Daniel Sergile

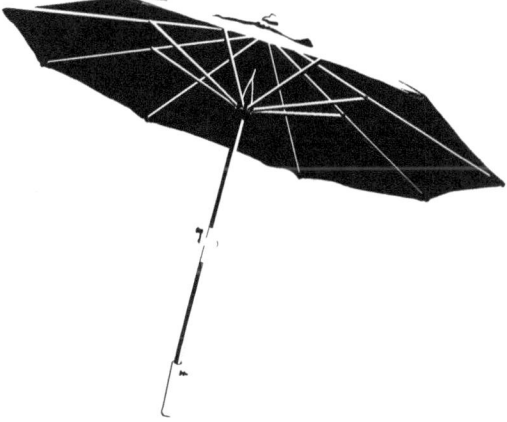

Umbrella 2
Tommy Bradley

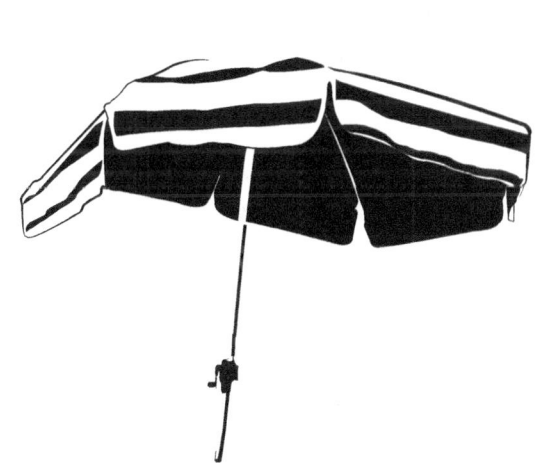

Umbrella 4
Sarah Petti

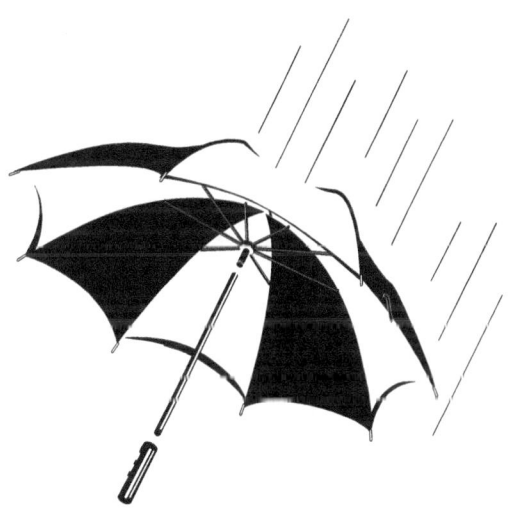

Umbrella 1
Yael Rotstein

Bicycle

Will Miller

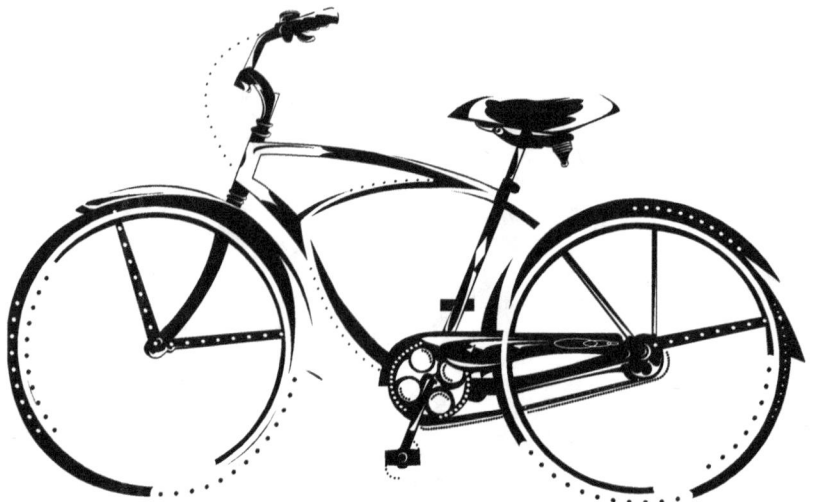

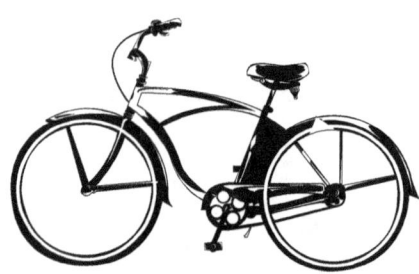

Bicycle
Will Miller

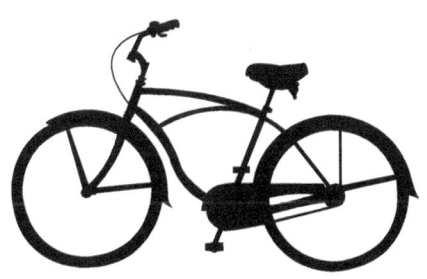

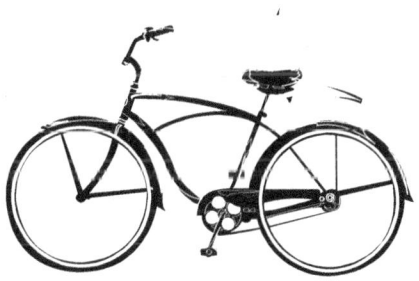

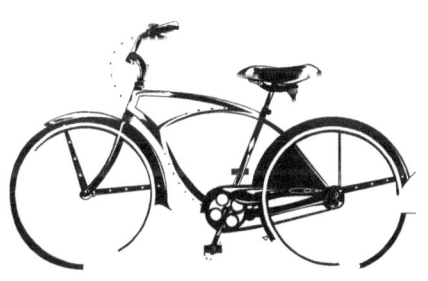

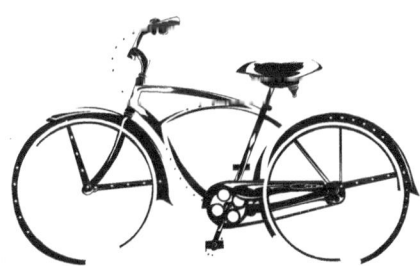

Blender
Ryan Meis

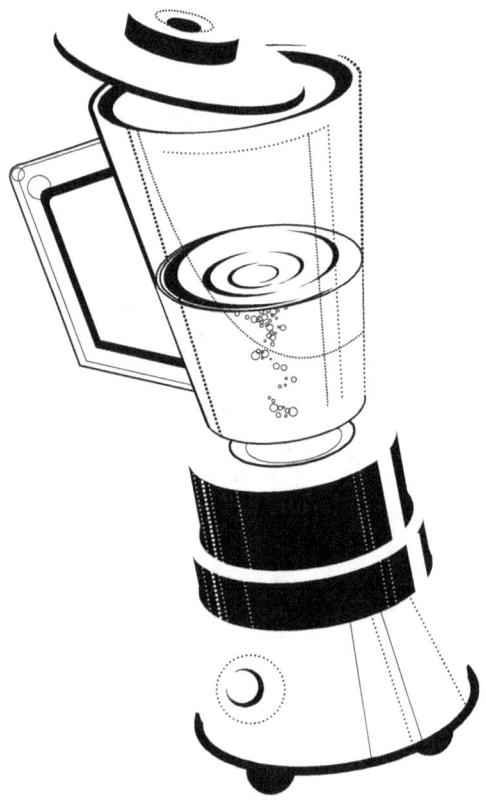

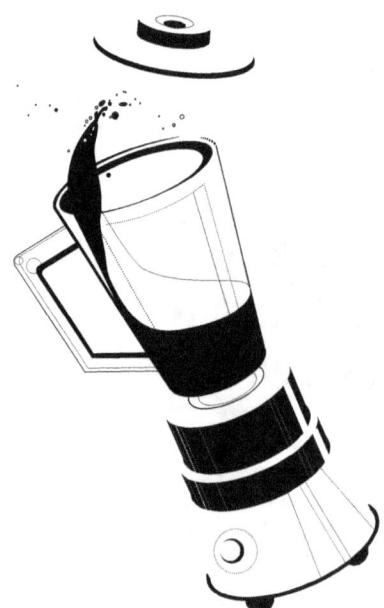

Function
The blender seems to come to life through the addition of the visual suggestion of liquid and movement. The dynamic quality is intensified by placing the drawing on the diagonal so as to appear to be tipping.

Blender

Ryan Meis

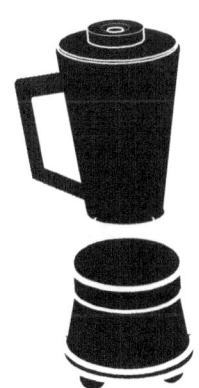

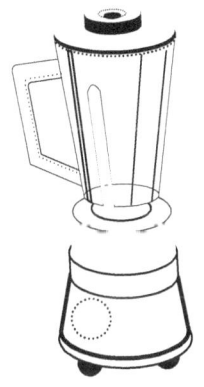

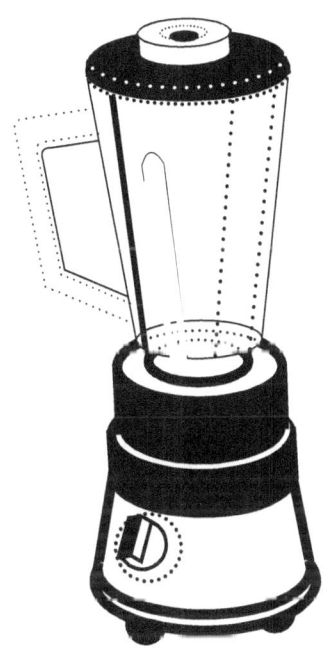

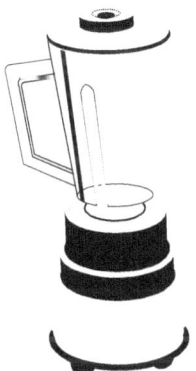

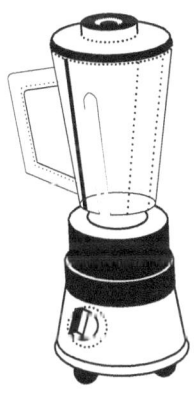

Boat Motor

Ronnie Koff

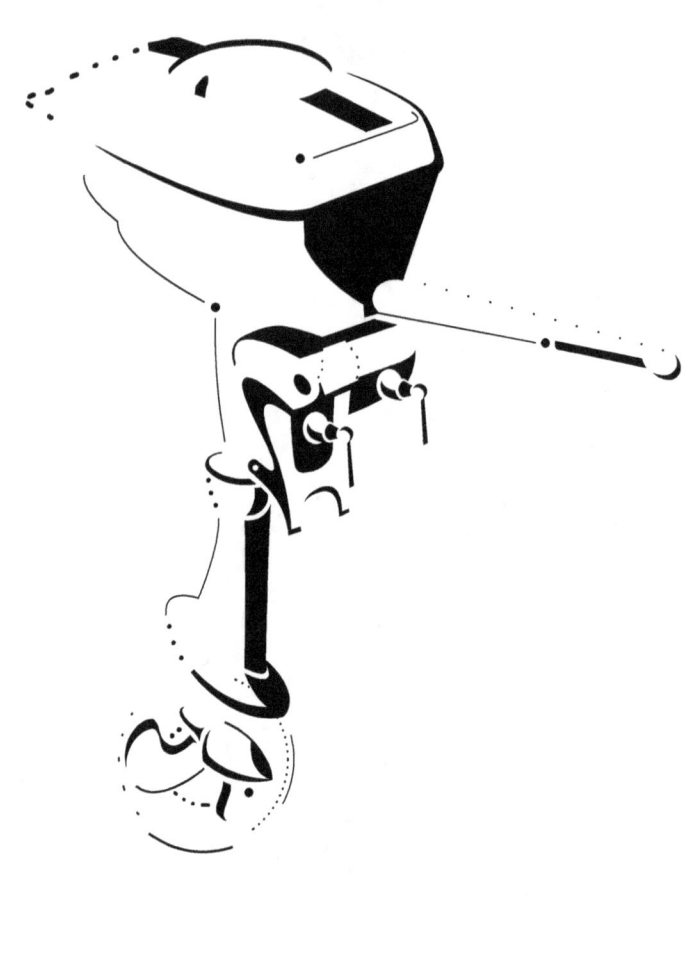

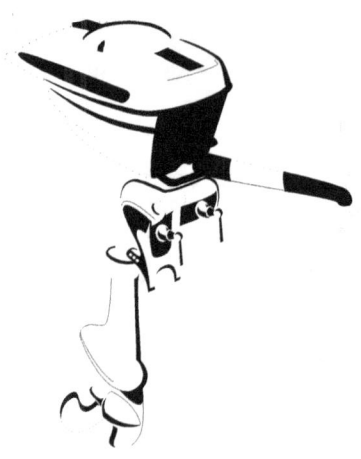

Boat Motor

Ronnie Koff

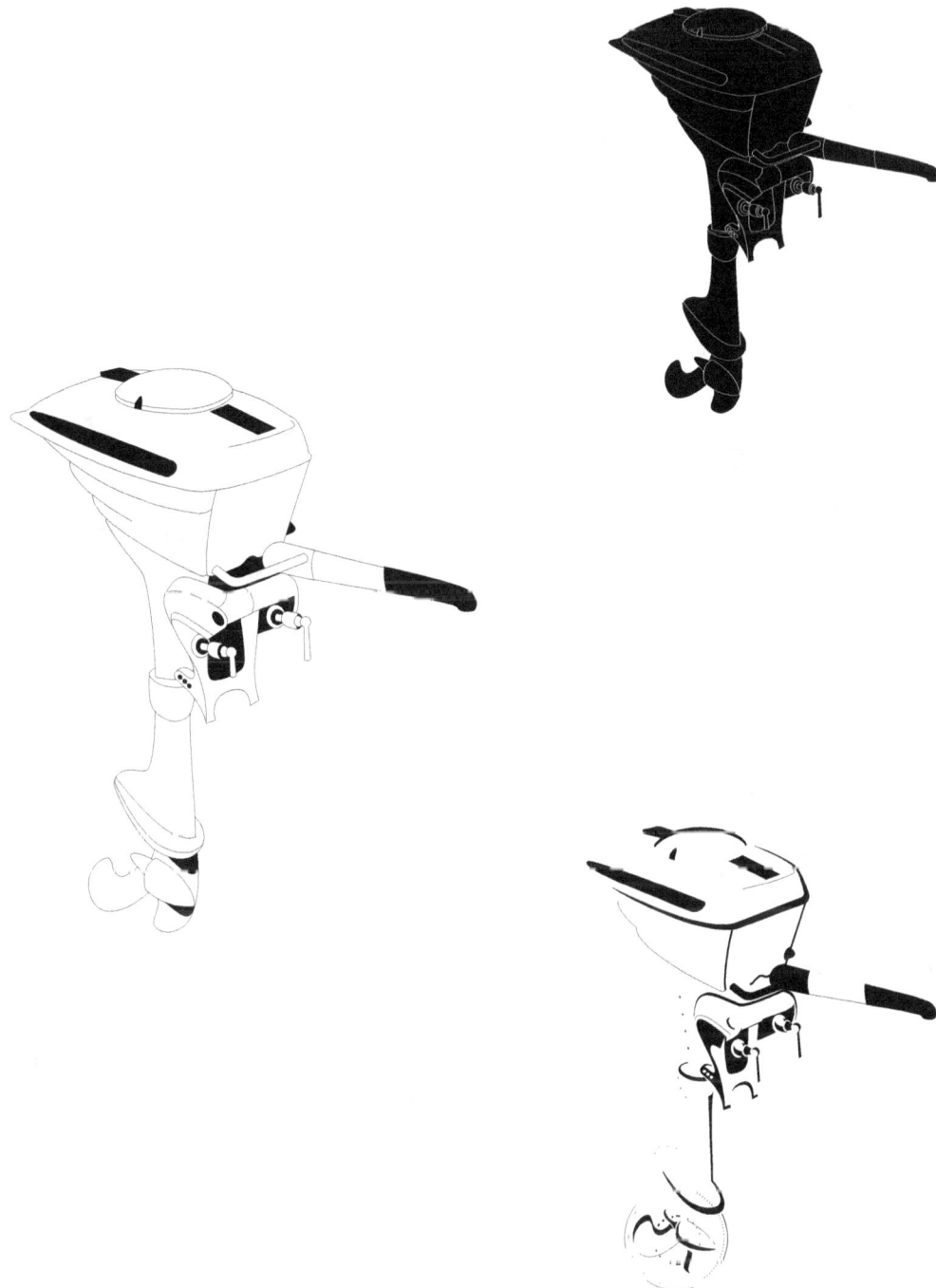

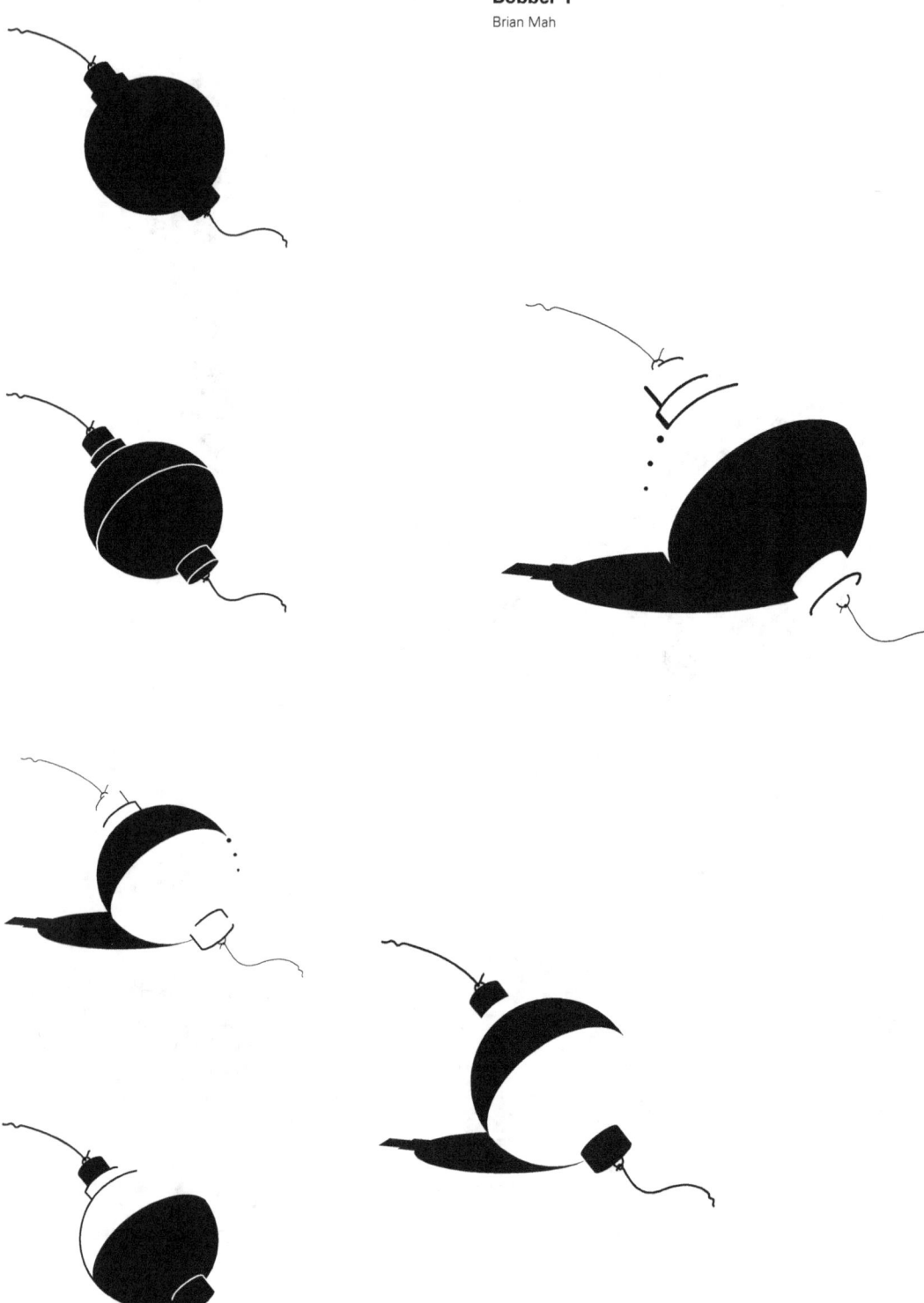

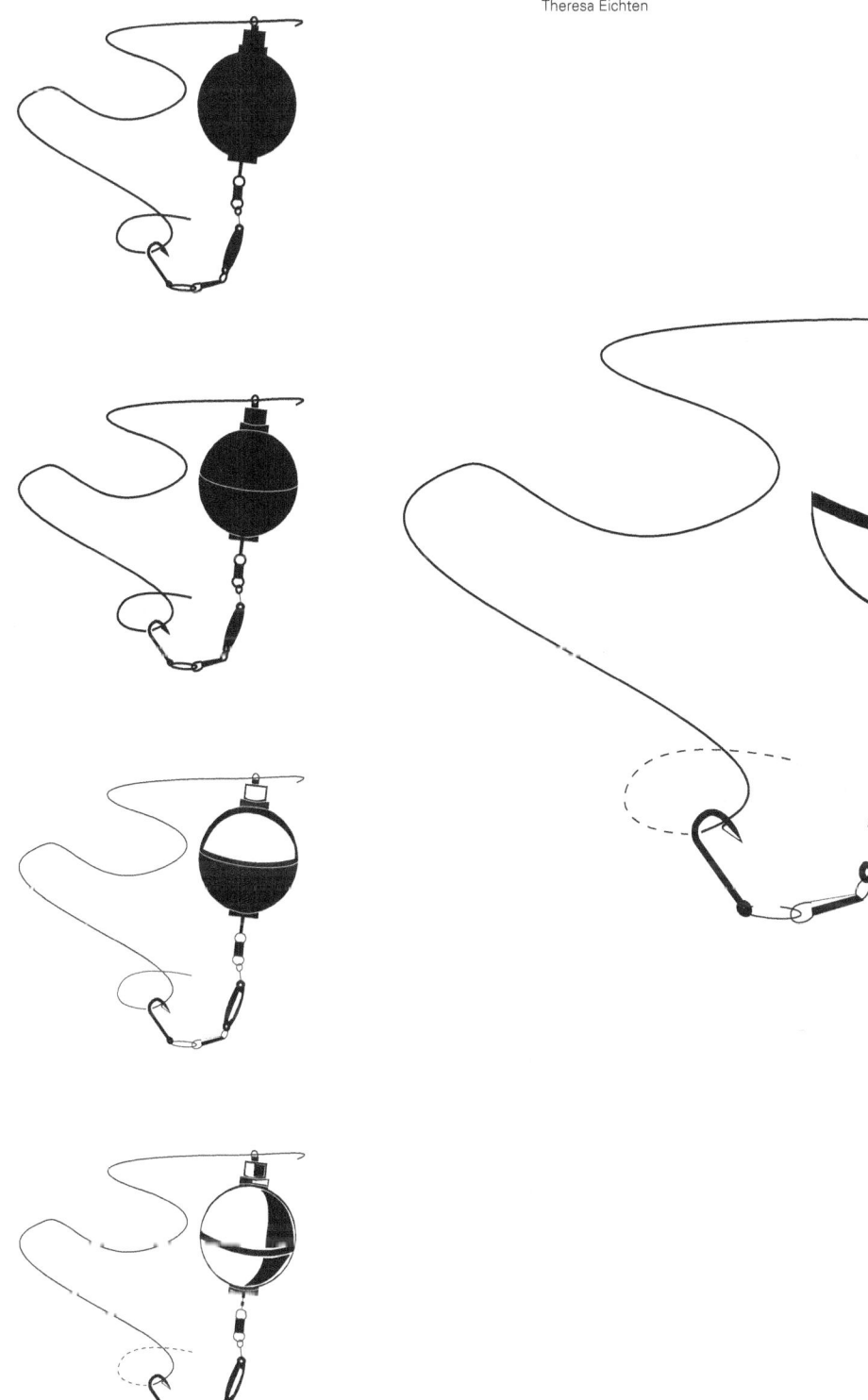

37

Brush

Heather Clark

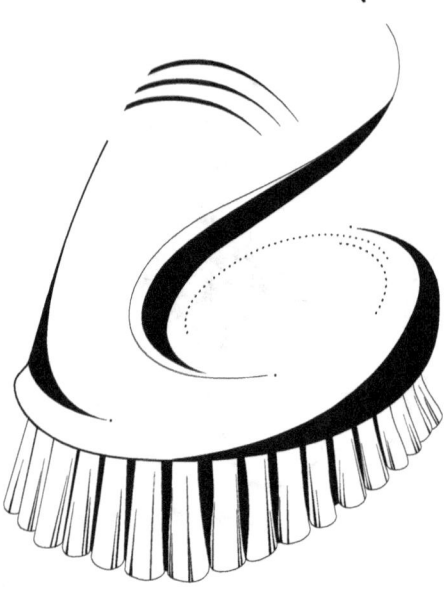

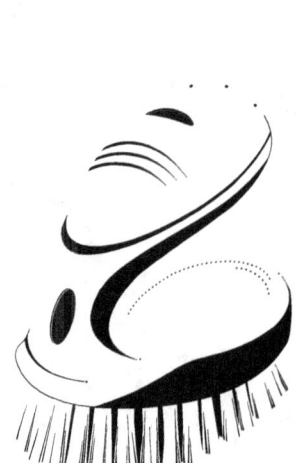

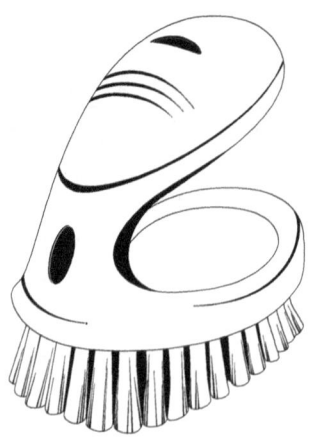

Brush

Heather Clark

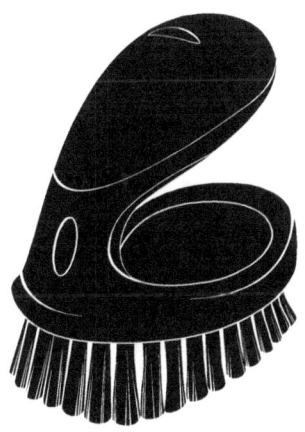

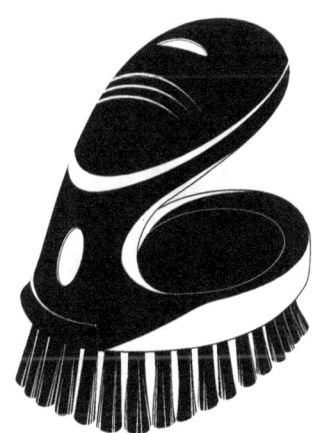

Exploratory hand-graphic drawing series.

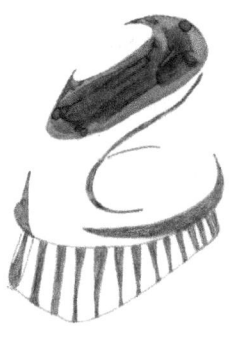

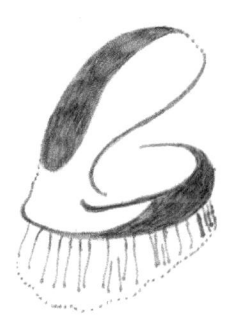

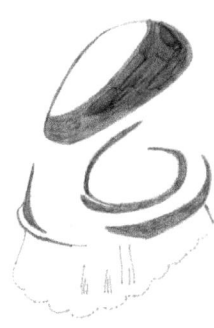

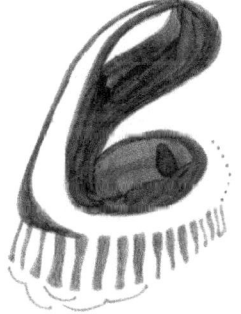

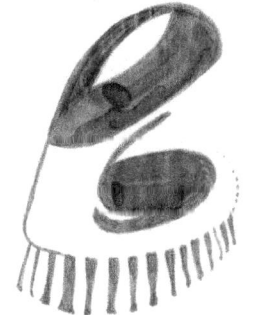

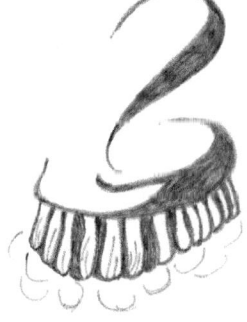

Ceiling Fan
Jeremy Kennedy

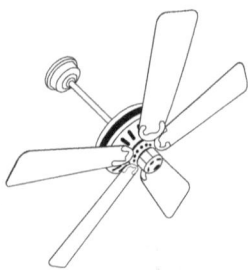

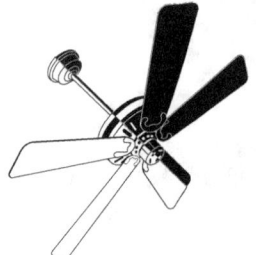

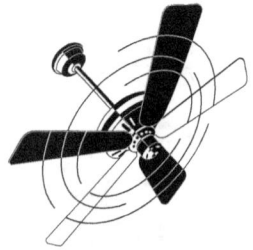

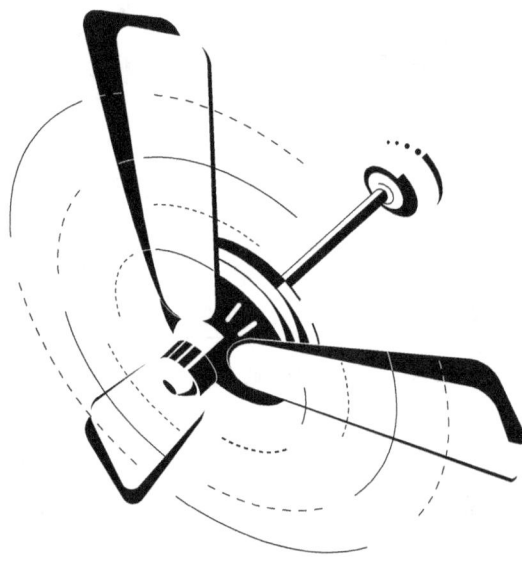

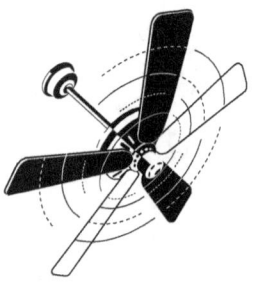

Angle and Movement

The diagonal placement of the ceiling fan emphasizes the dynamic movement of the blades. The use of wide and narrow dashes as well as rhythmical broken lines is an interesting communication of wind and motion. The original fan consisted of five blades and the final translation has three blades so as to simulate the optical characteristics of a swiftly rotating fan.

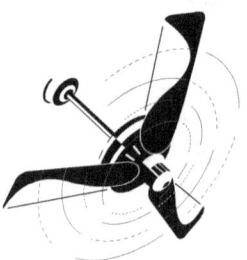

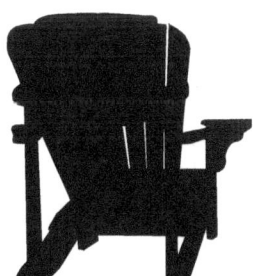

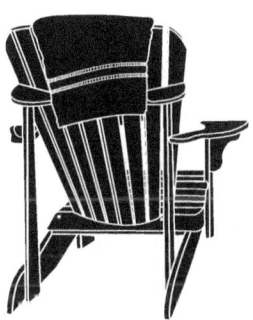

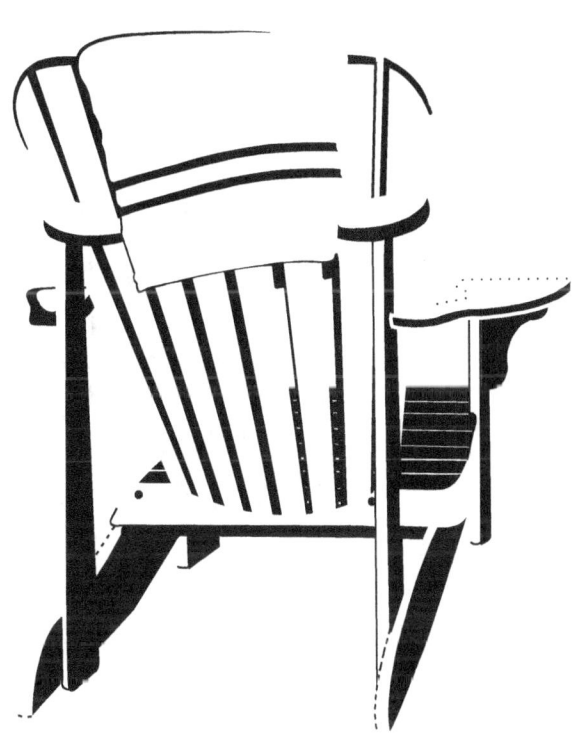

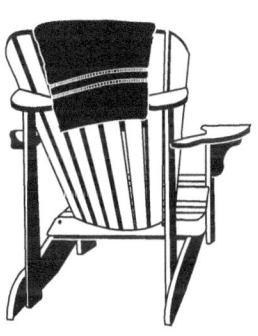

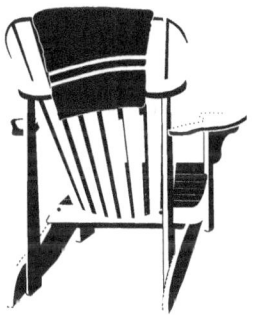

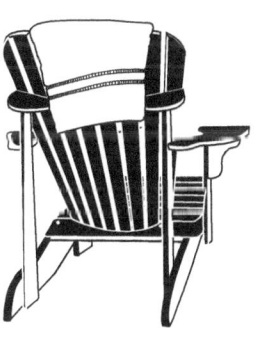

Clock

Chris Haslup

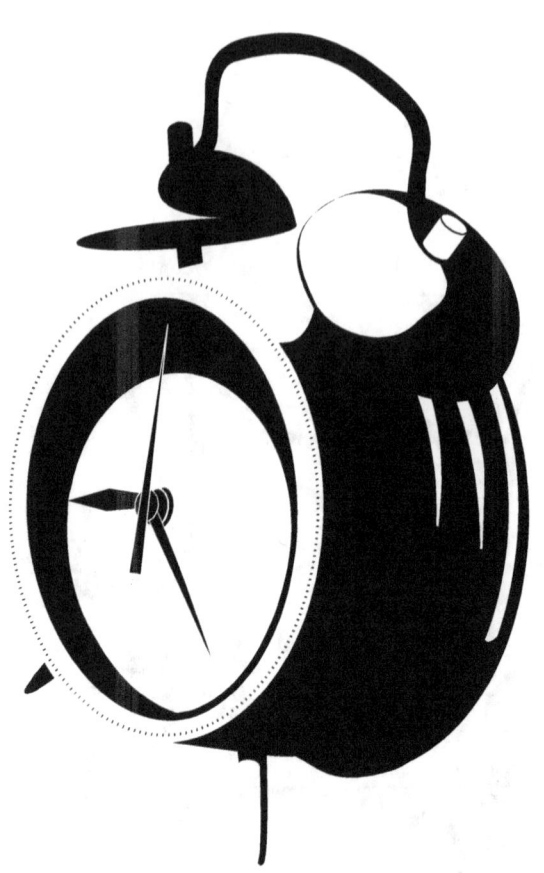

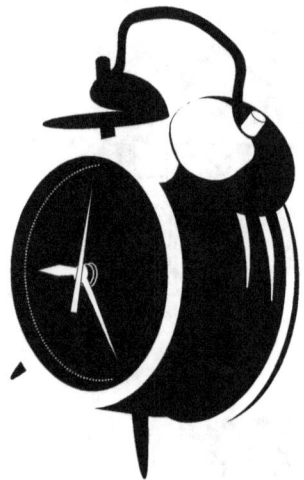

Clock

Chris Haslup

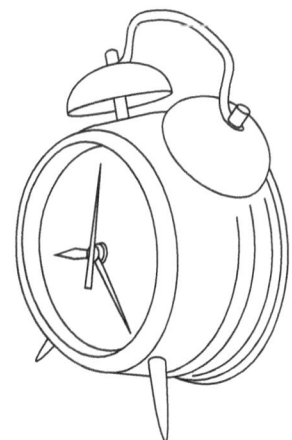

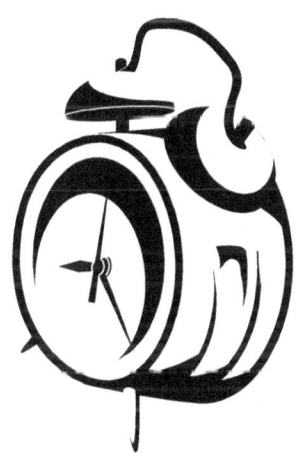

Exploratory hand-graphic drawing series.

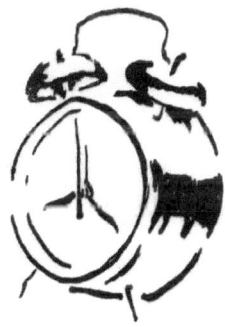 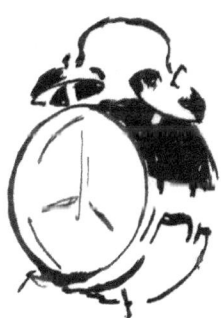 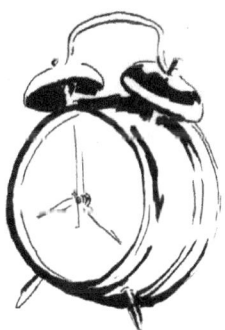 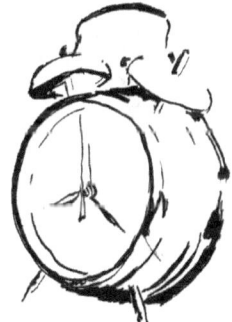

Coke Bottle
Cassia Dominguez

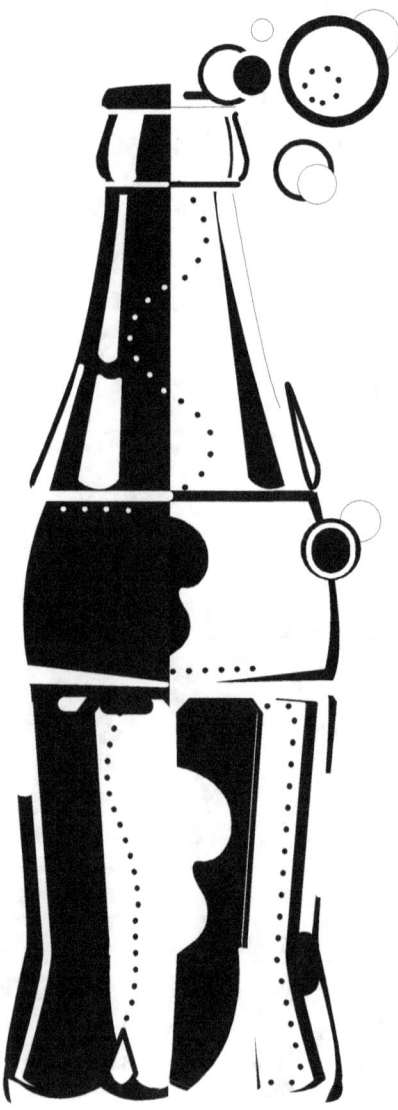

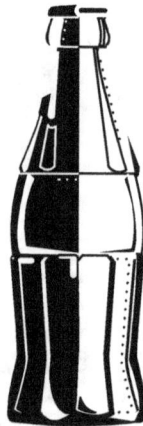

Effervescence
The distinctive form of the coke bottle makes it
an interesting graphic translation subject. In addition to graphically translating the faceted bottle,
the designer also abstracted and illustrated the
effervescence of the product.

Coke Bottle
Cassia Dominguez

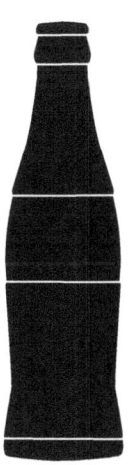

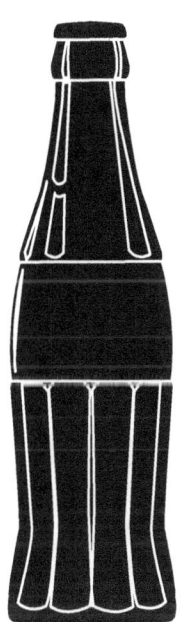

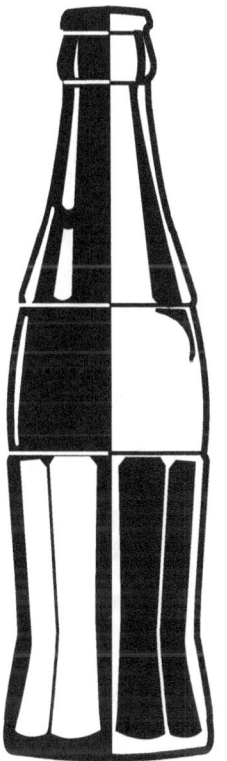

Earbuds

Joseph Kiem Vu

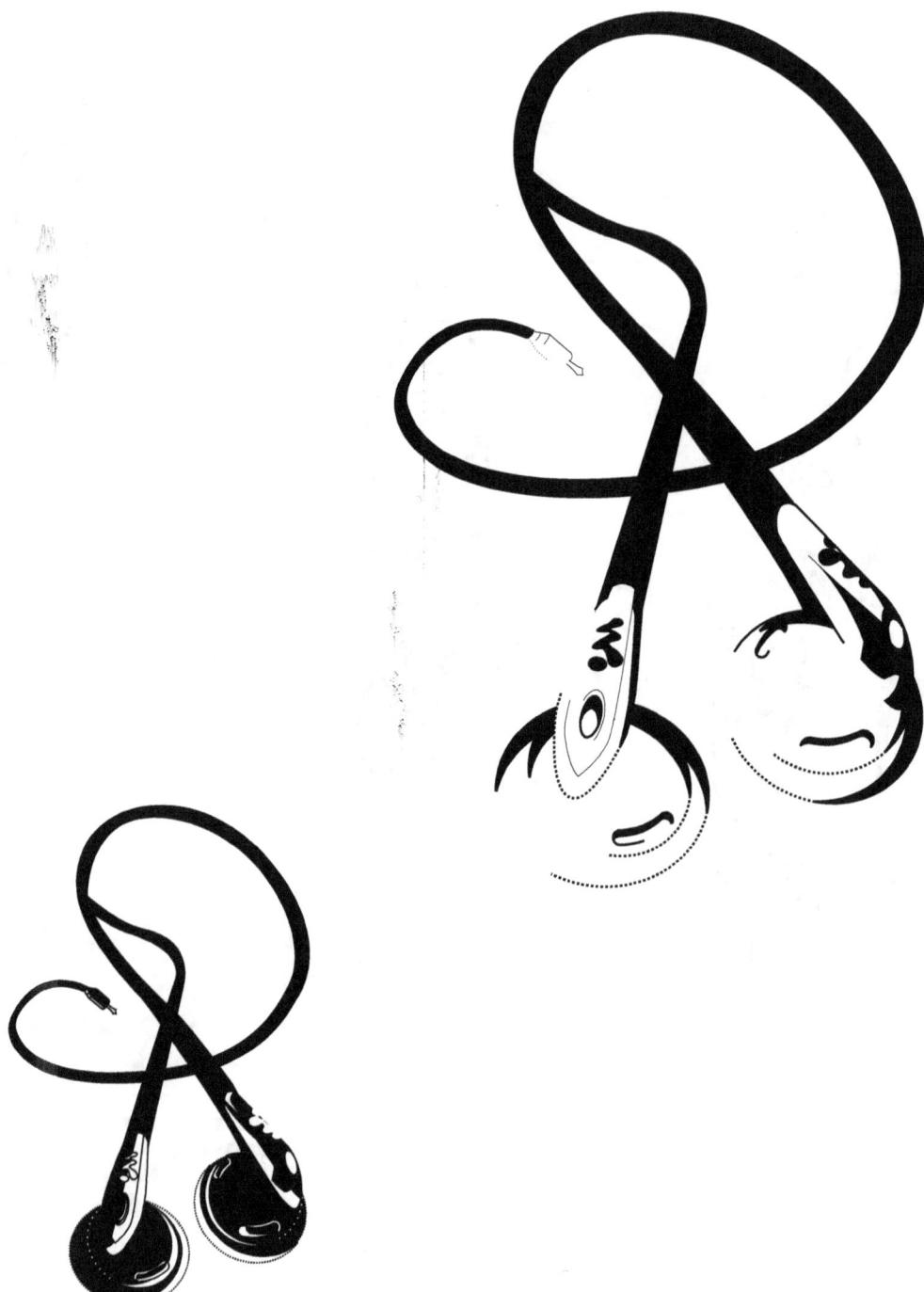

Earbuds
Joseph Kiem Vu

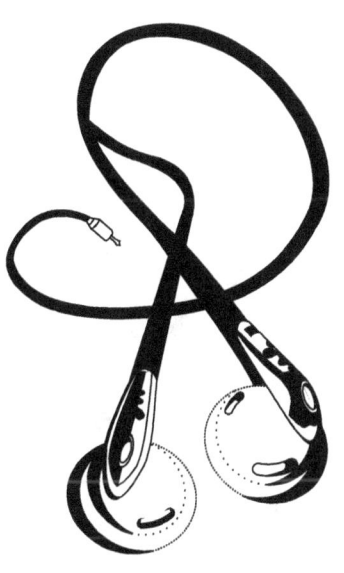 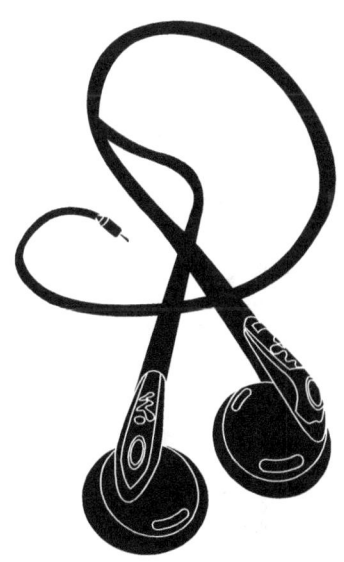

Exploratory hand-graphic drawing series.

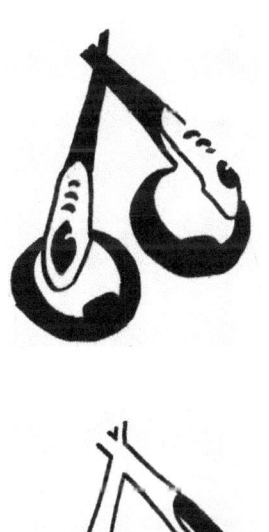 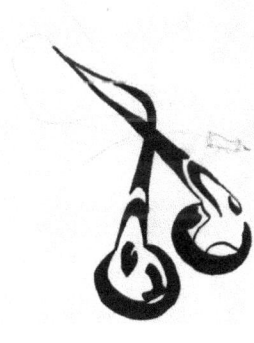

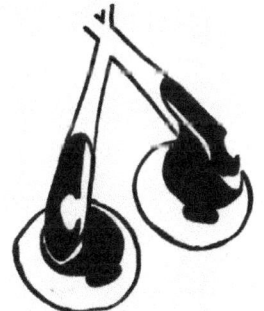 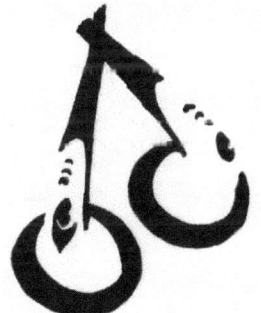 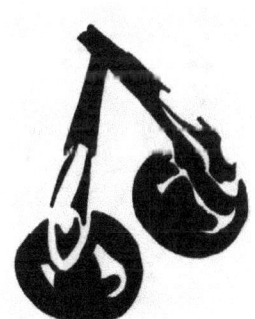

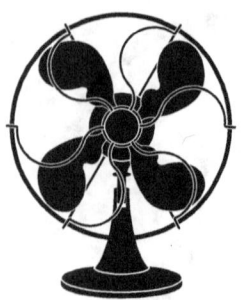

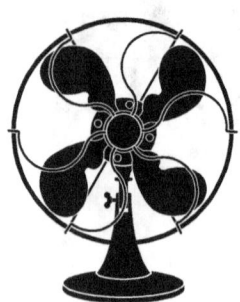

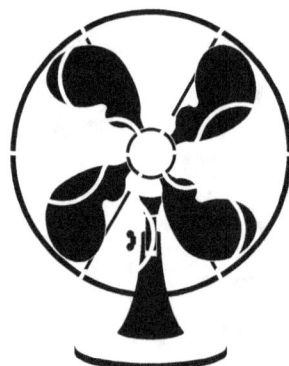

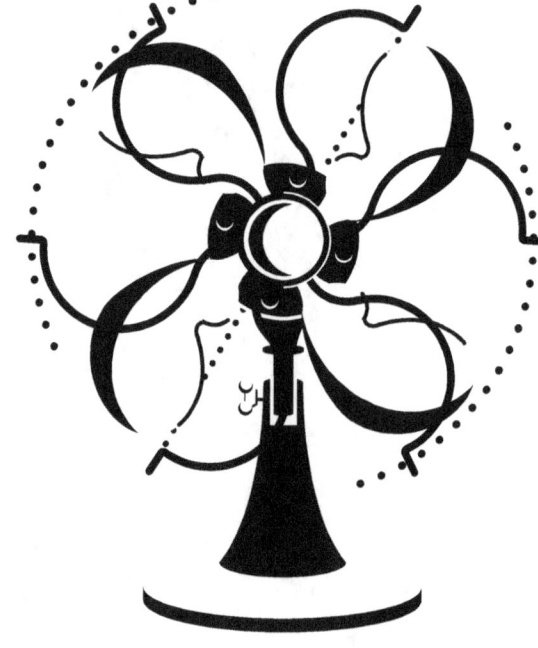

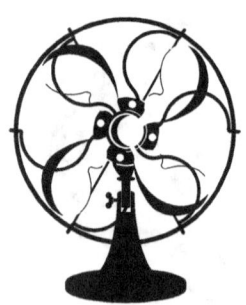

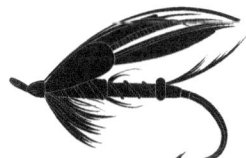

Fishing Lure
Jana Dee Bassingthwaite

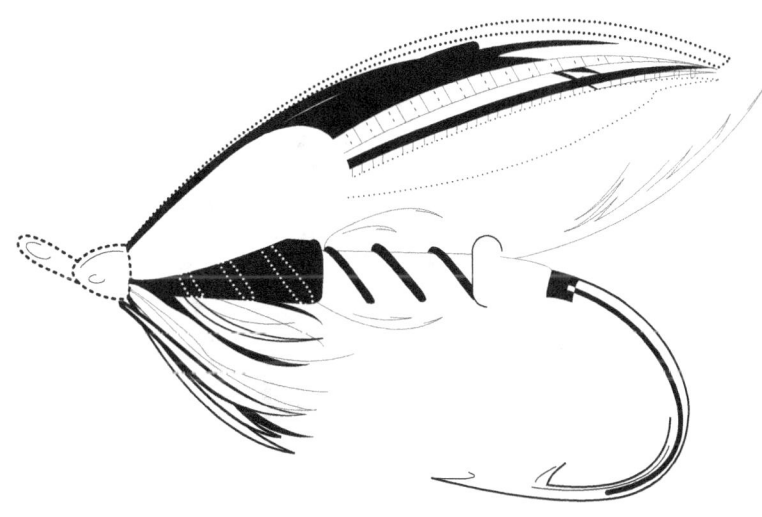

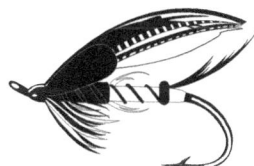

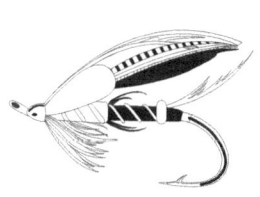

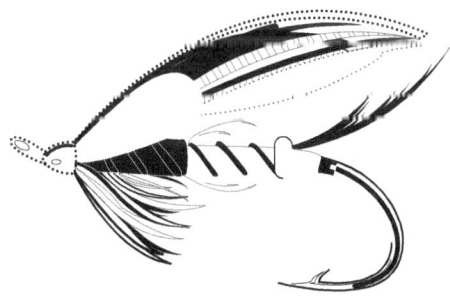

Fishing Reel

Jason Richardson

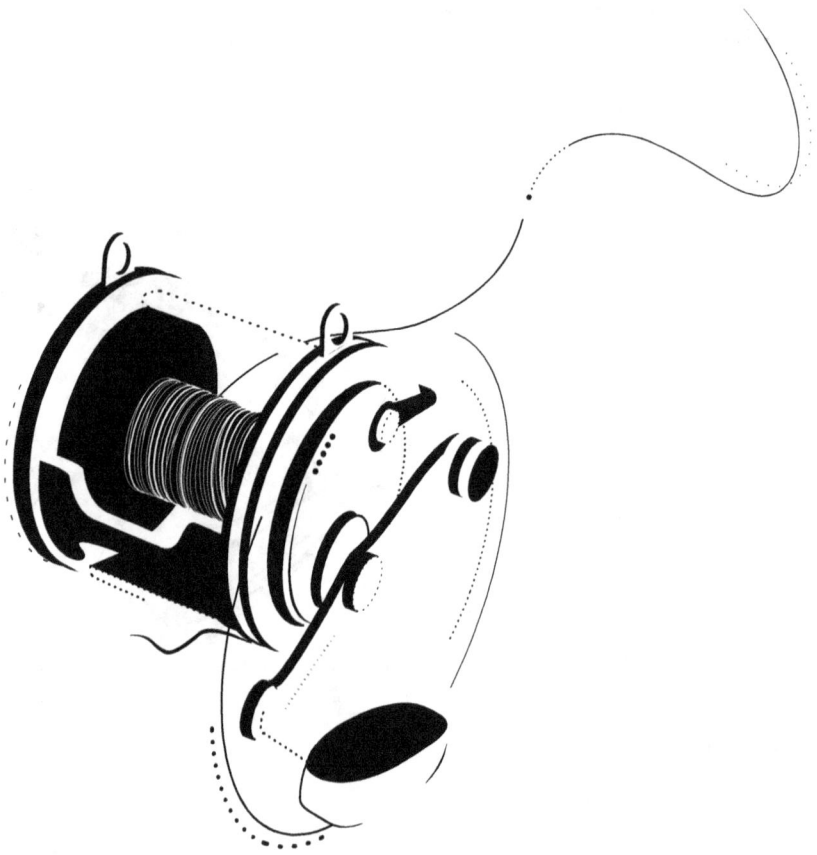

Aural Connotations
The initial fishing reel drawings are complex and well crafted but static. The final study employs more closure and the visual suggestion of movement. This visual suggestion of the movement of the handle and play of the line also evokes the aural connotation of whirring sound making the drawing all the more dynamic.

Fishing Reel

Jason Richardson

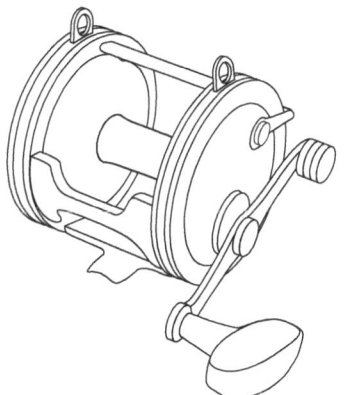

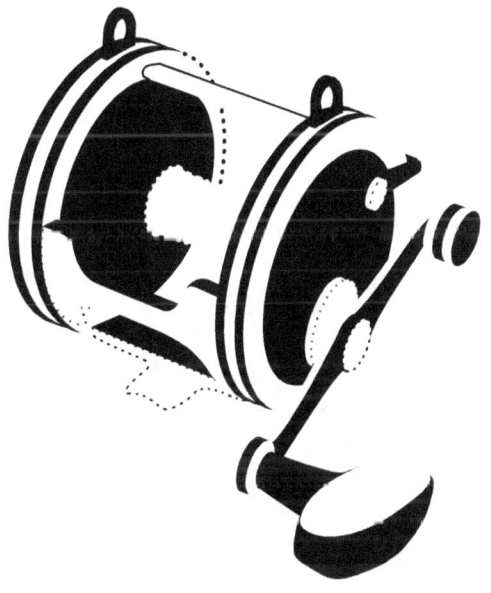

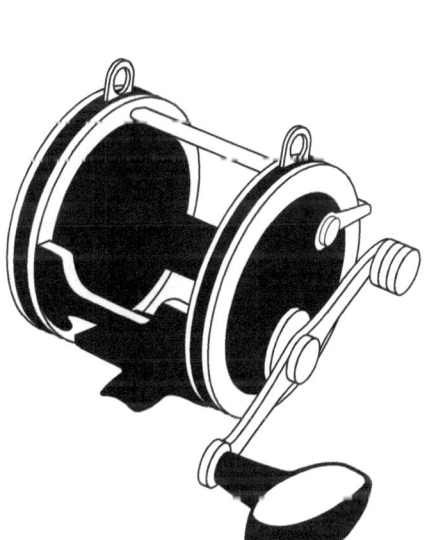

French Horn

Jeremy Cox

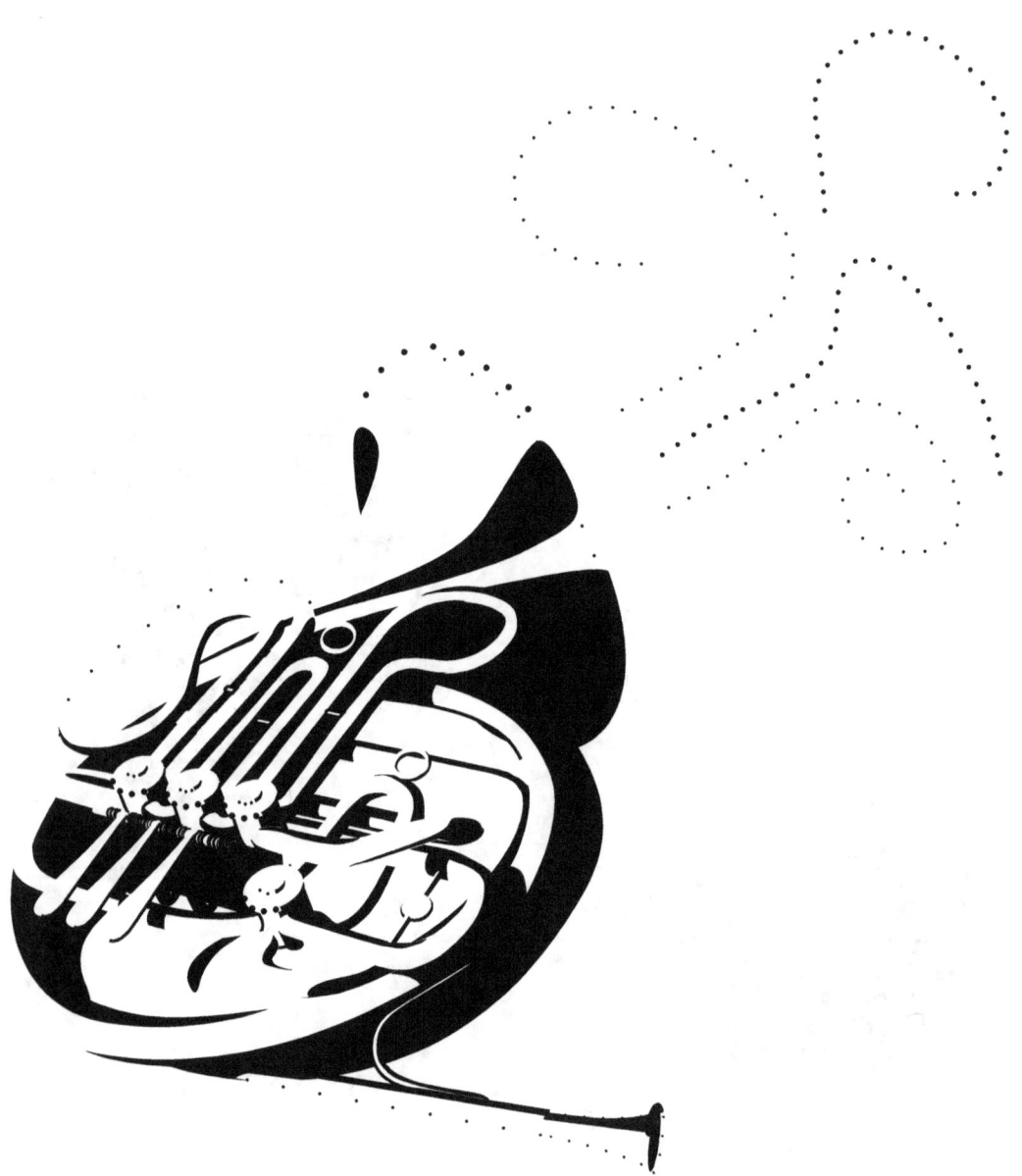

French Horn

Jeremy Cox

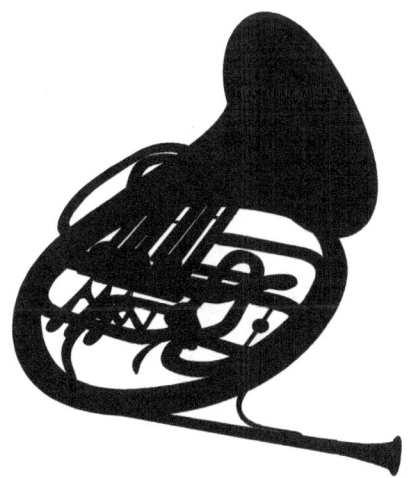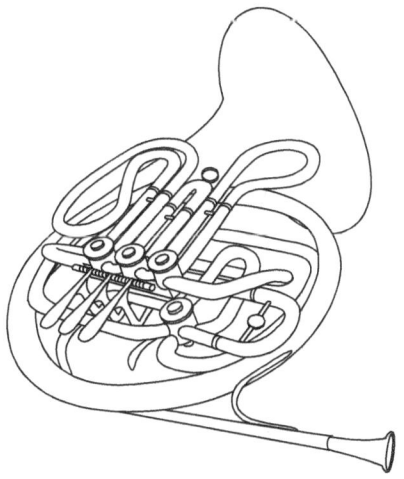

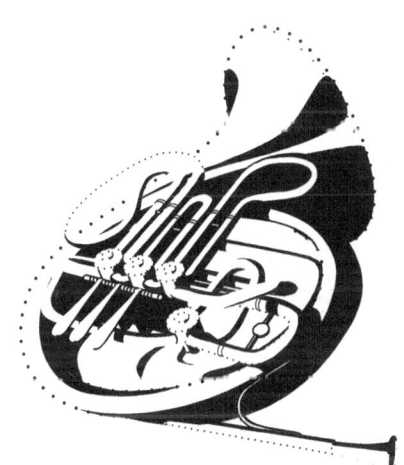

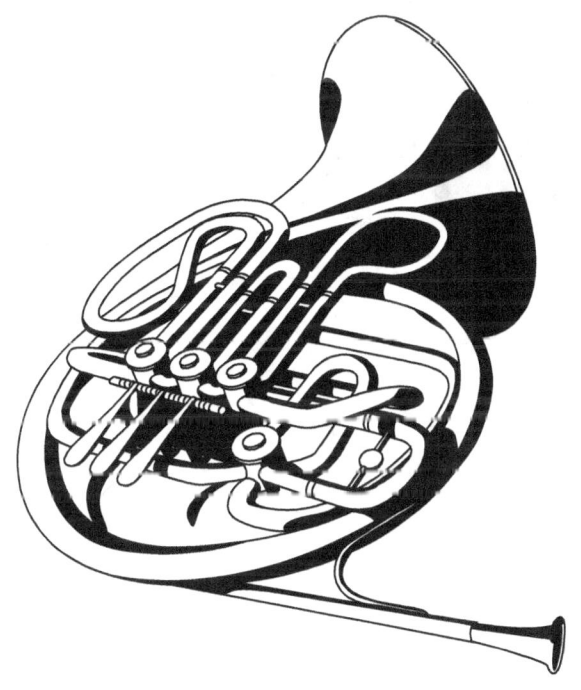

Gas Mask
Heidi Dyer

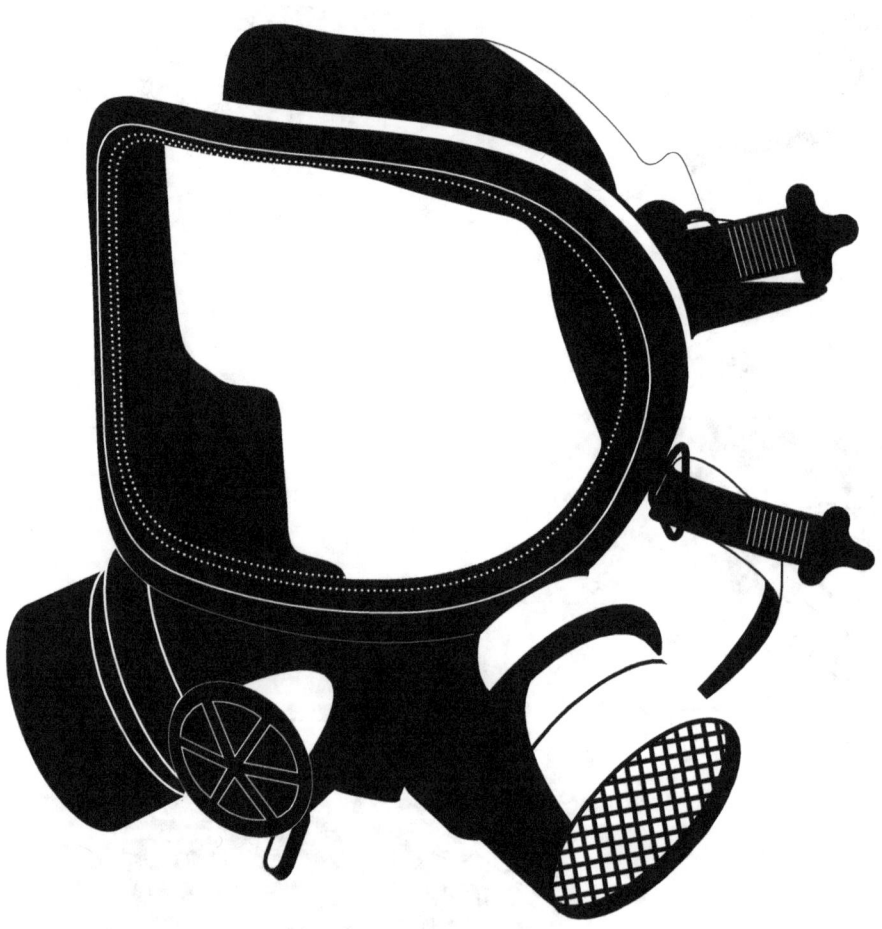

Gas Mask
Heidi Dyer

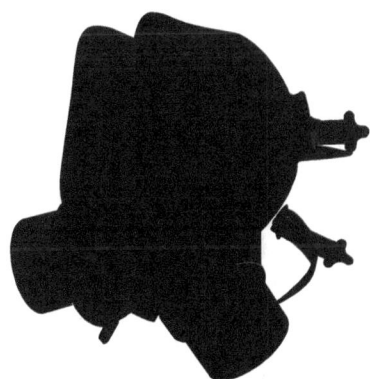

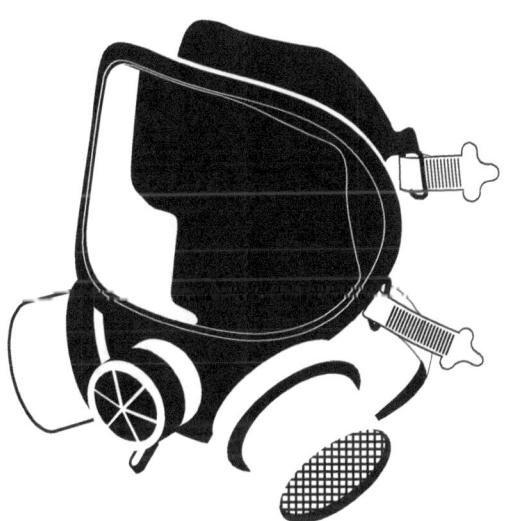

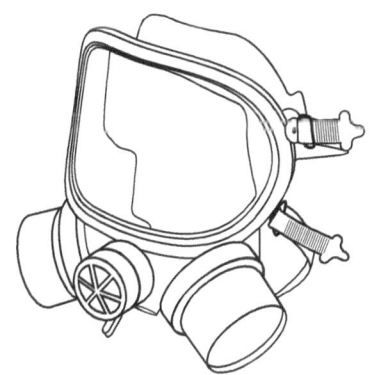

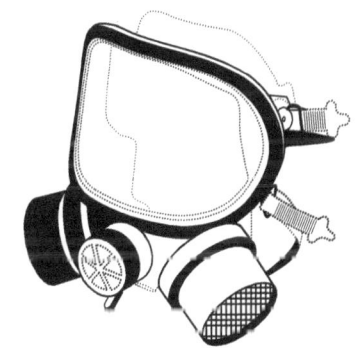

Guitar Series

The guitar series features drawings of a single object with a number of different individual interpretations. Each designer is challenged to draw and graphically translate the guitar. All of the designers found the rhythm and repetition of dots and dashes to be evocative of the strumming music made by the guitar.

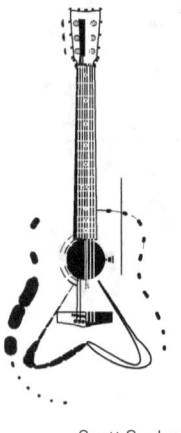

Scott Suplee

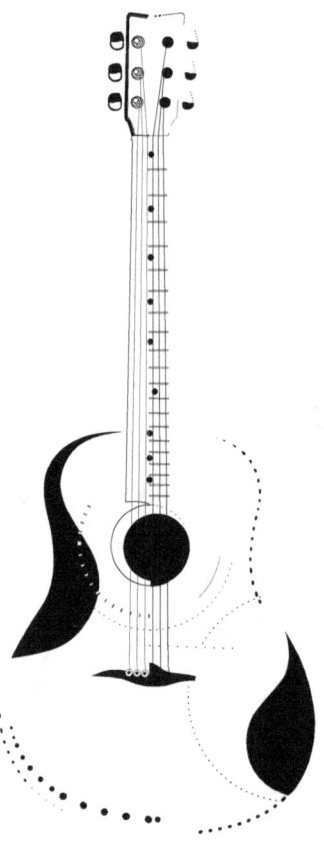

Jared Ponchot

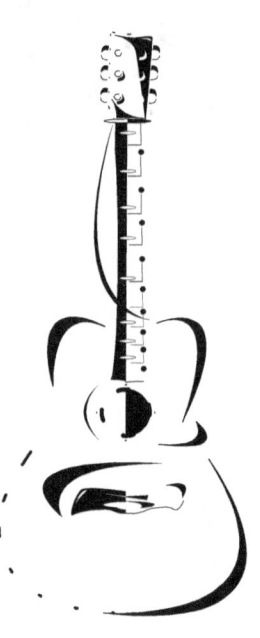

Will Miller

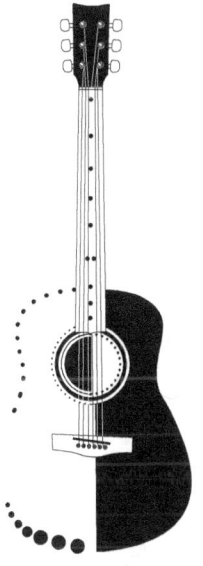

Arthur Gilo

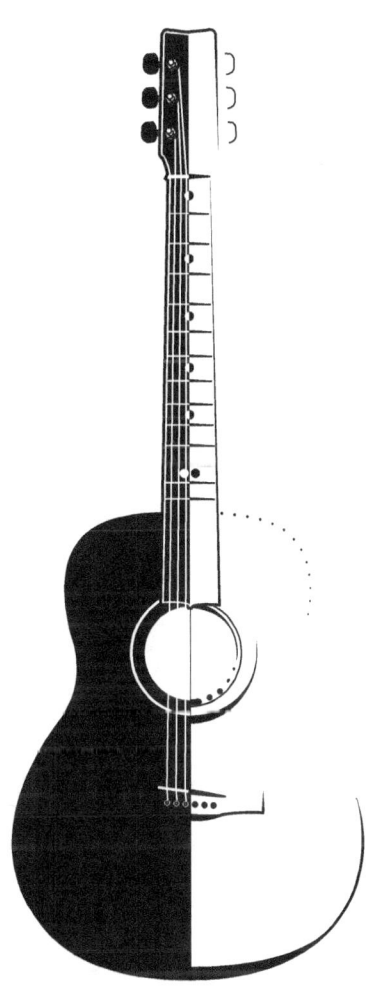

Jared Ponchot

Mike Osgood

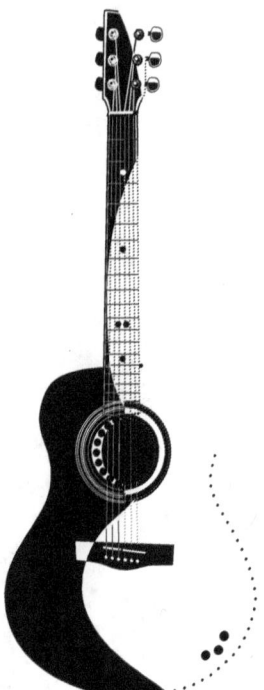

Neva Morris

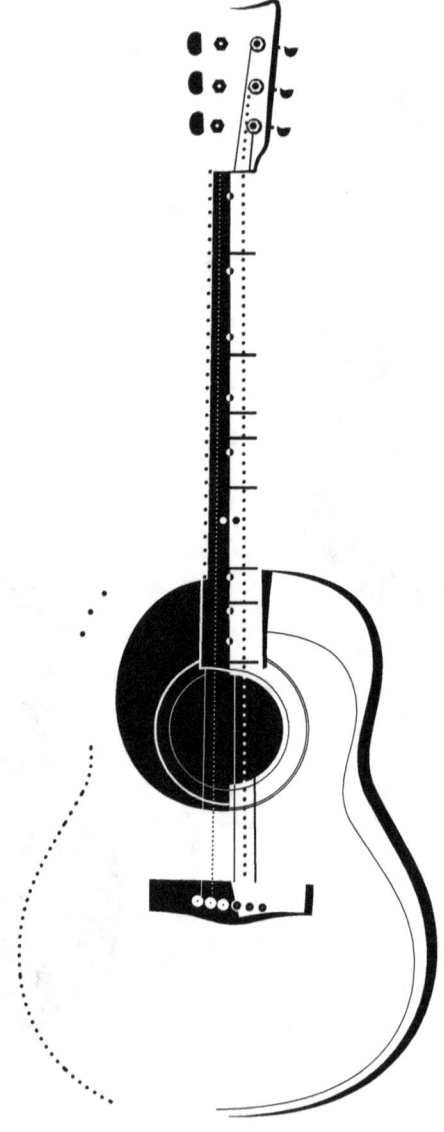

Ronnie Koff

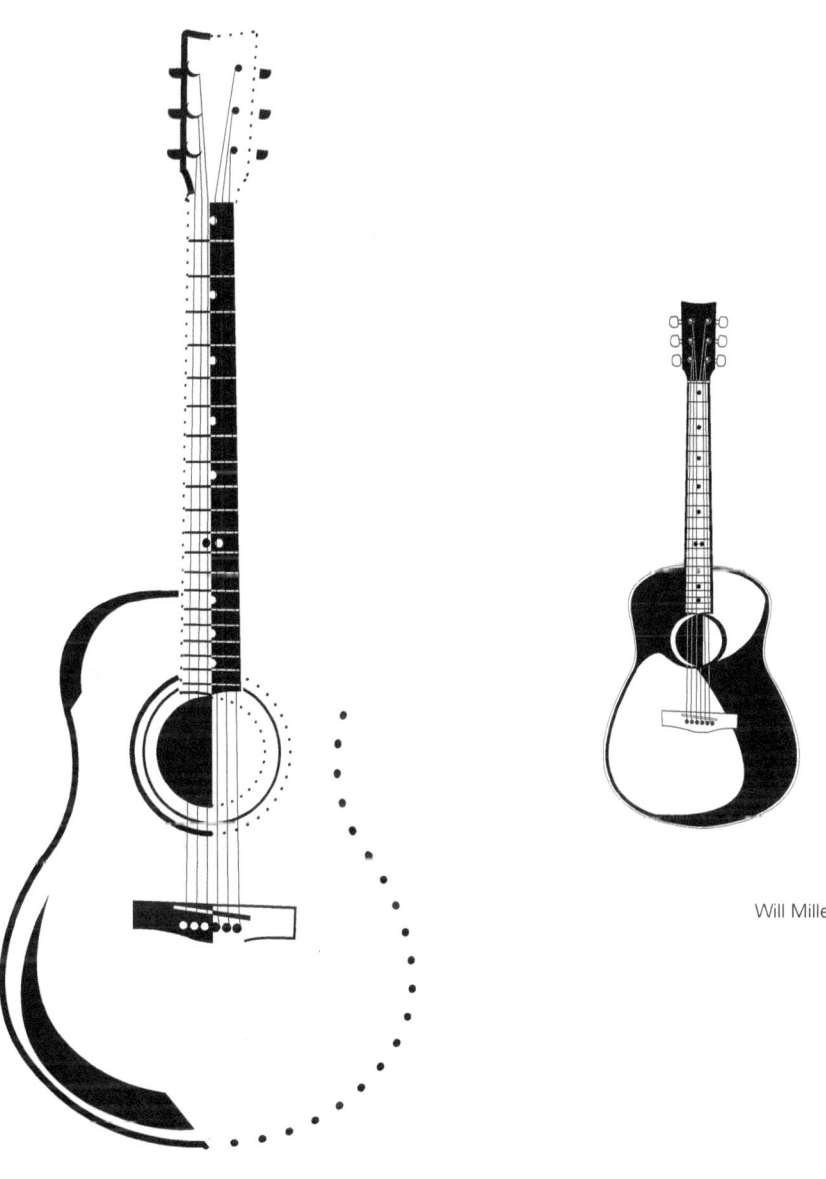

Will Miller

Wood D. Wobor

Guitar Series
Glen Bowman II, Sara Waterman

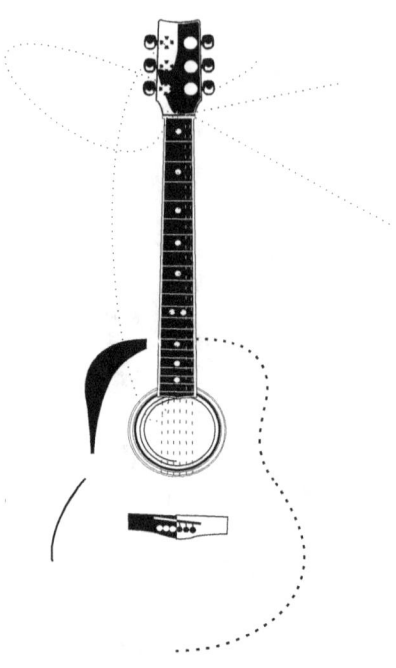

Glen Bowman II

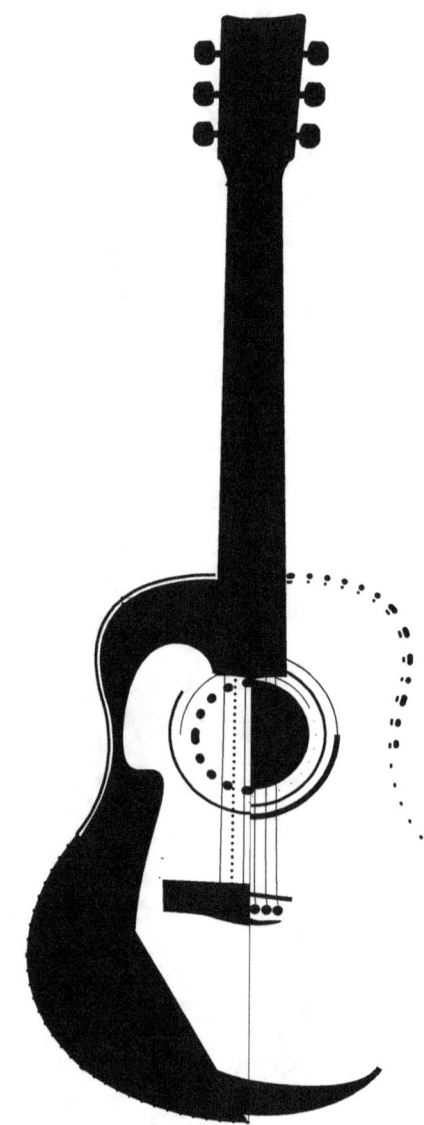

Sara Waterman

Guitar Series
Drew Tyndall, Mark Unger, Glen Bowman II

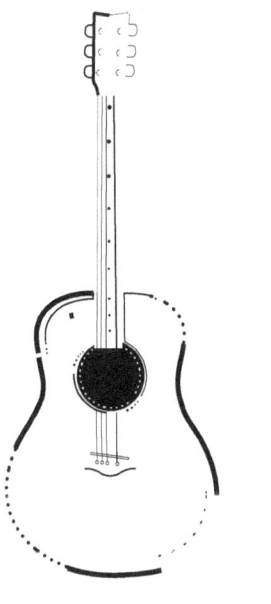

Drew Tyndell

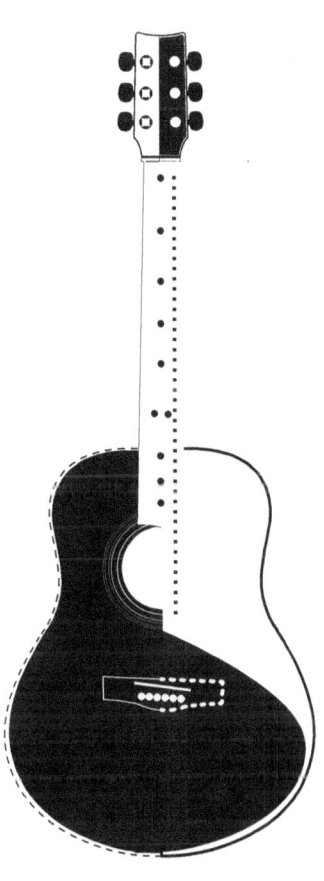

Glen Bowman II

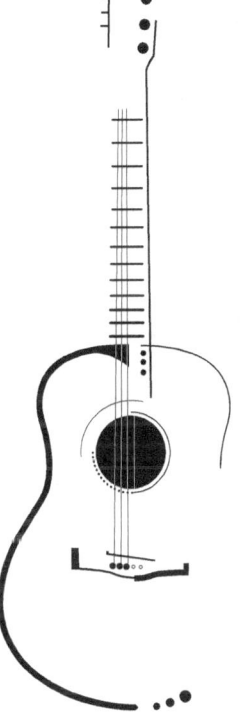

Mark Unger

Headphones

Jose Rodriguez

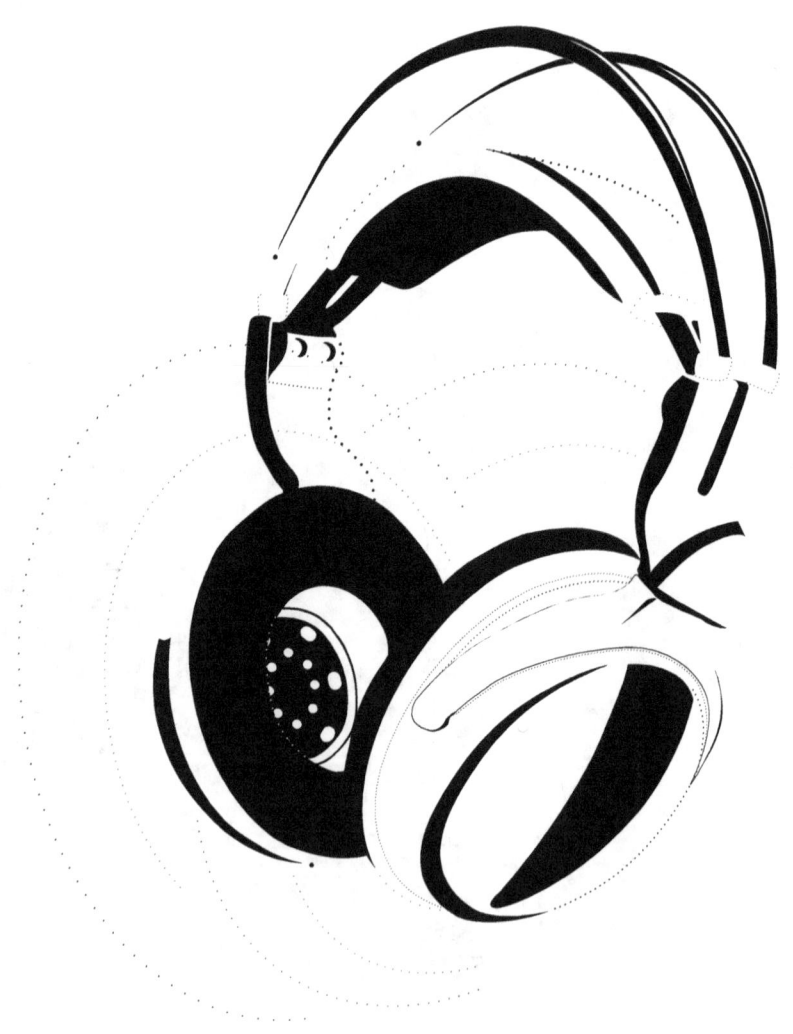

Headphones
Jose Rodriguez

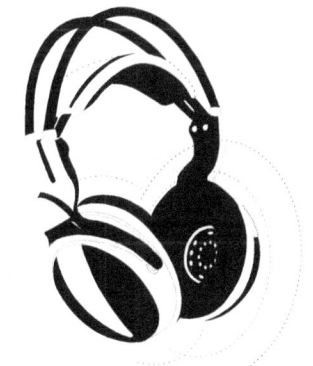

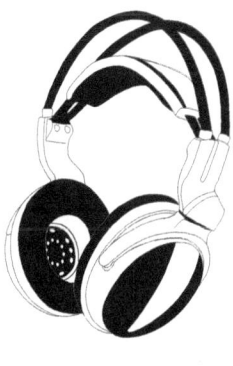

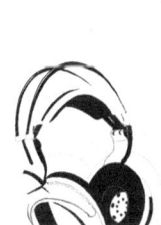

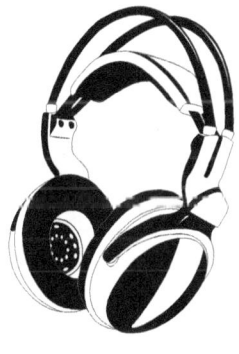

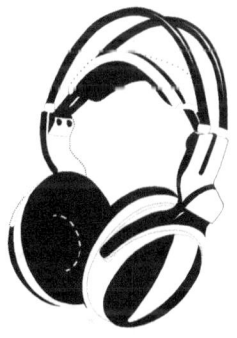

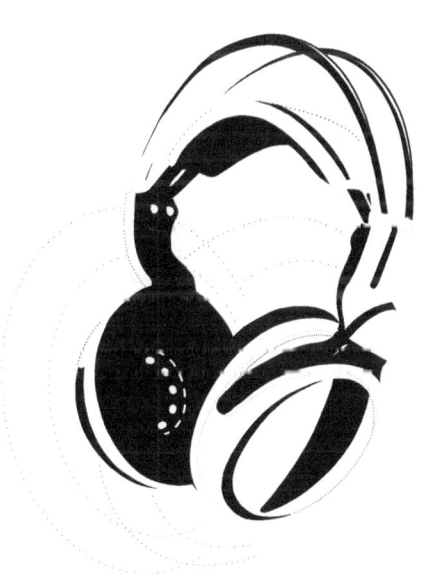

Juicer
Ronnie Koff

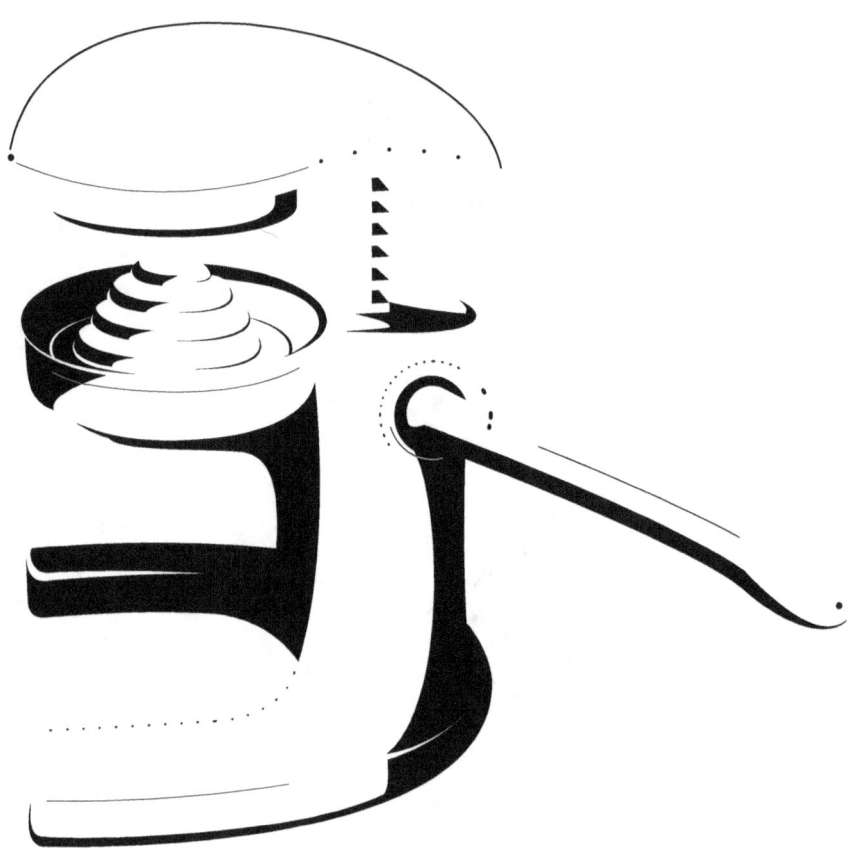

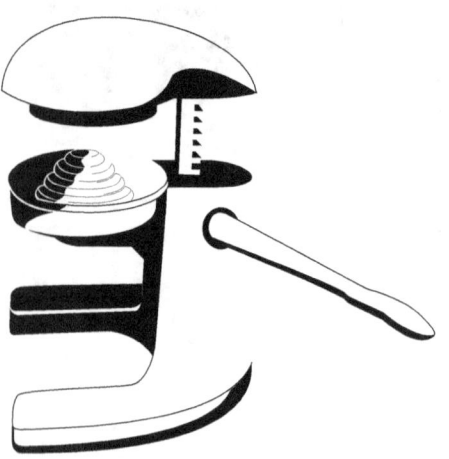

Repetition and Closure

Repetition and closure are two of the qualities that make this graphic translation of a juicer stunning. Areas of line are removed with just enough remaining to guide the mind's eye to complete the figure. The dots are far apart on the curvilinear top portion of the juicer creating a slow rhythm. They're closer together and then farther apart on the base of the handle creating a change in rhythm. Repetition is echoed in the tiered platform and ratchet device triangles.

Juicer

Ronnie Koff

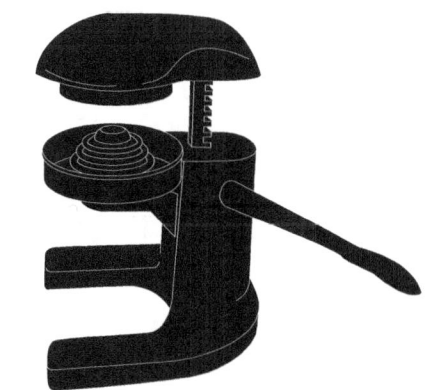

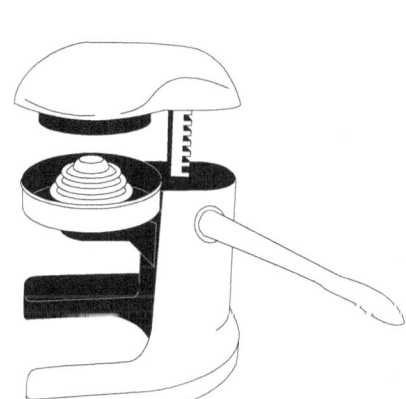

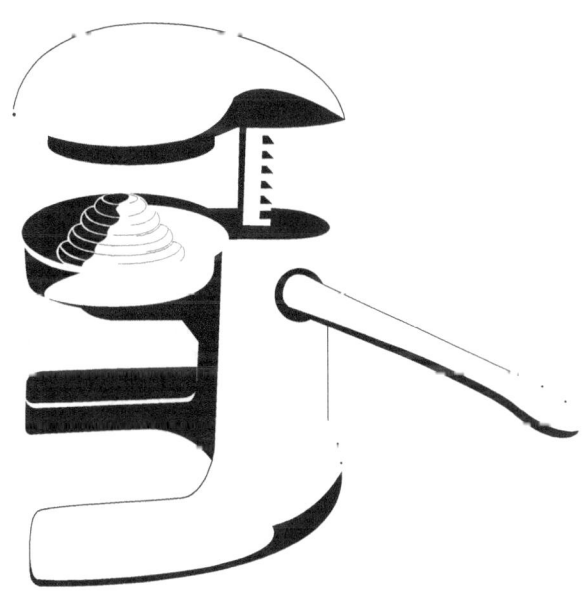

Movie Camera
Christopher Roeleveld

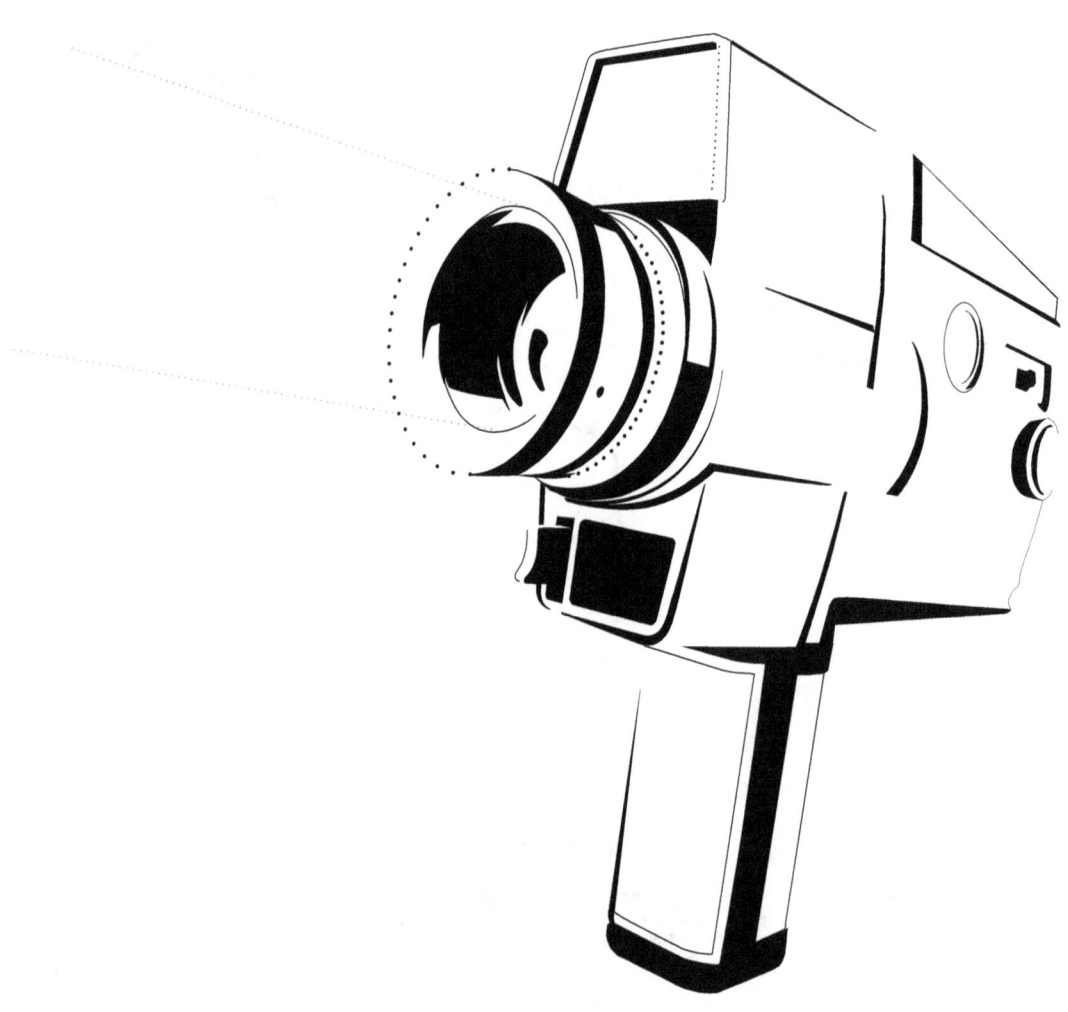

Movie Camera

Christopher Roeleveld

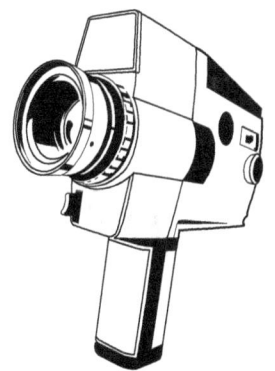

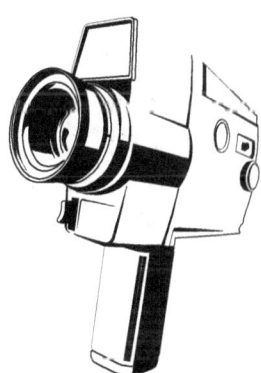

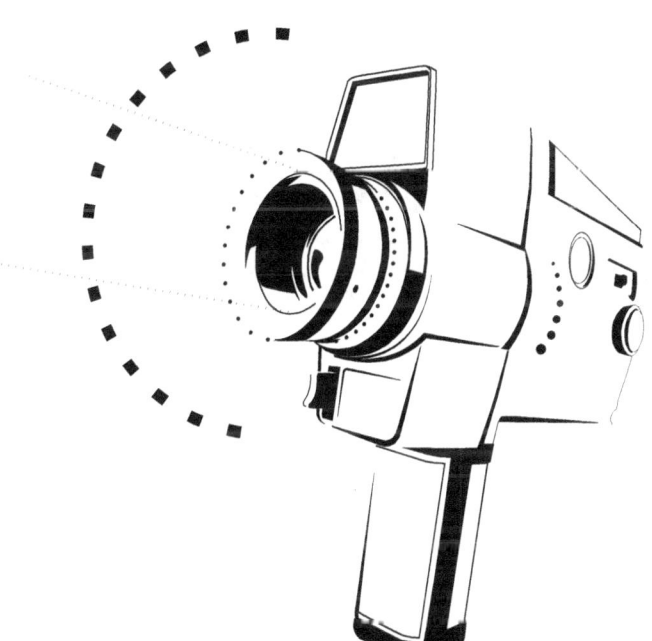

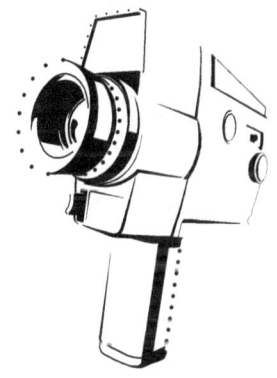

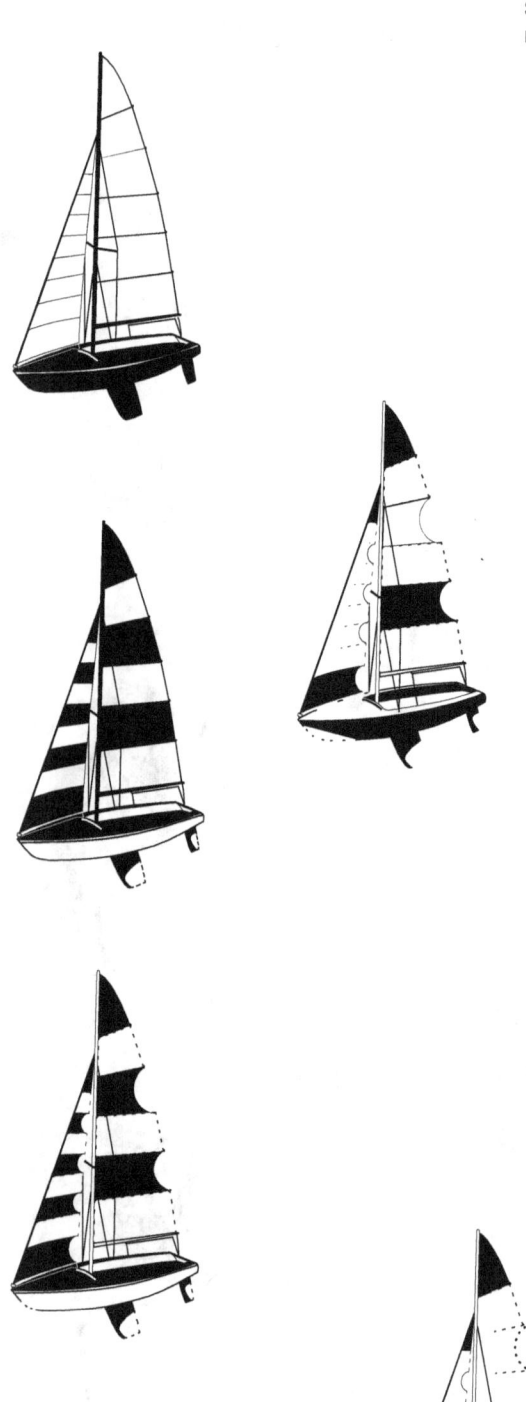

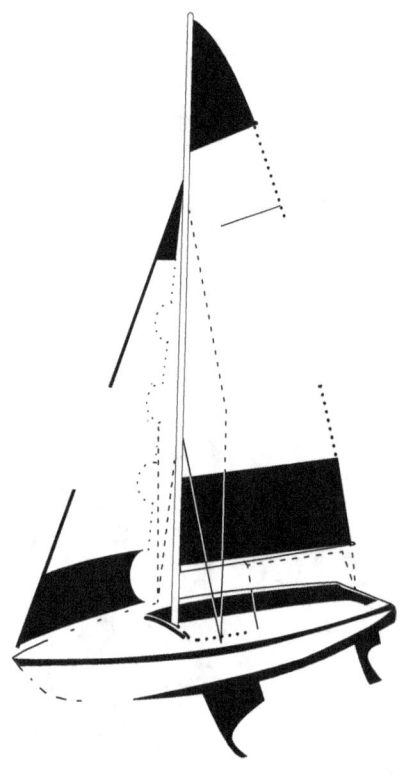

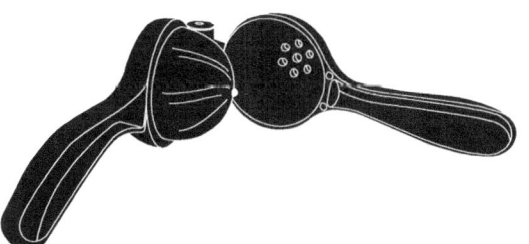

Squeezer

Michael Johnston

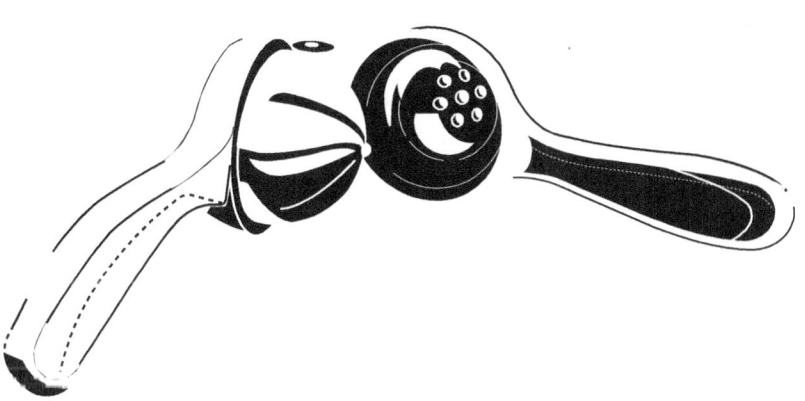

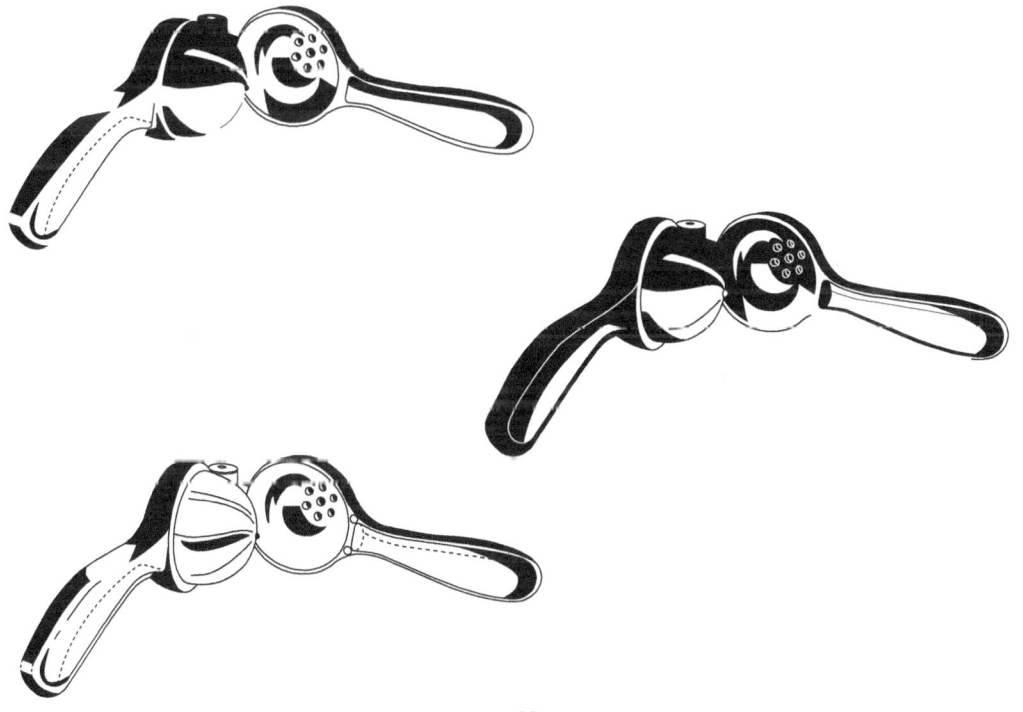

Sand Pail 1
Brian Curley

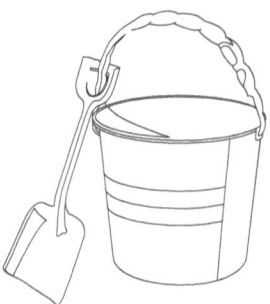

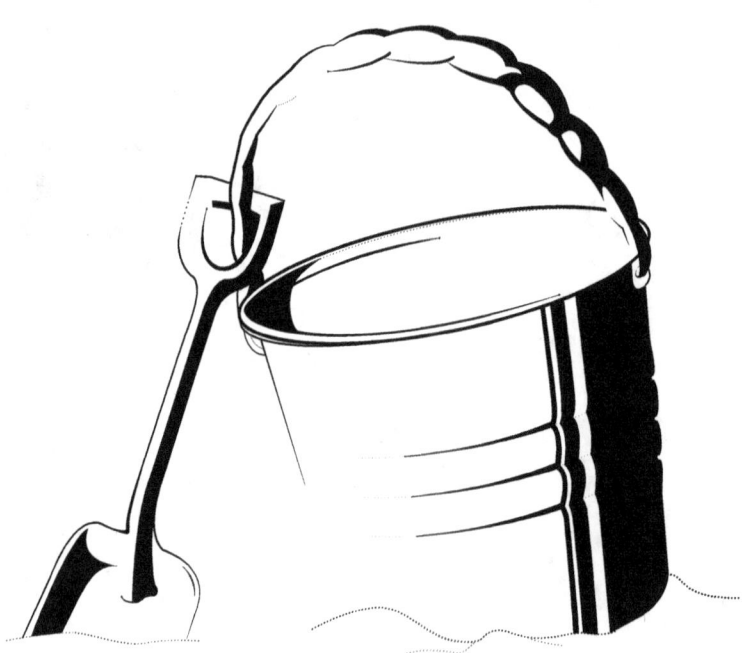

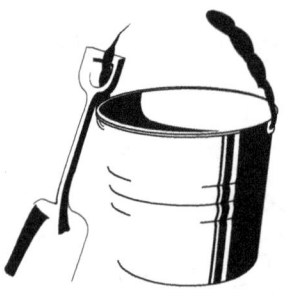

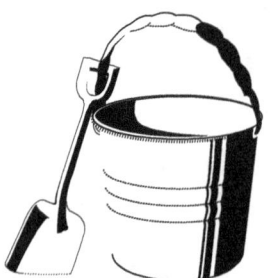

Sand Pail 2
Sarah Petti

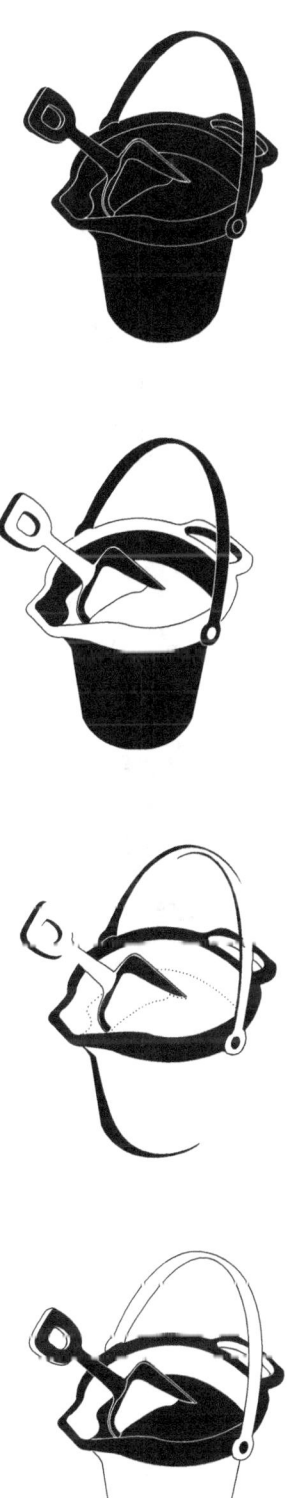

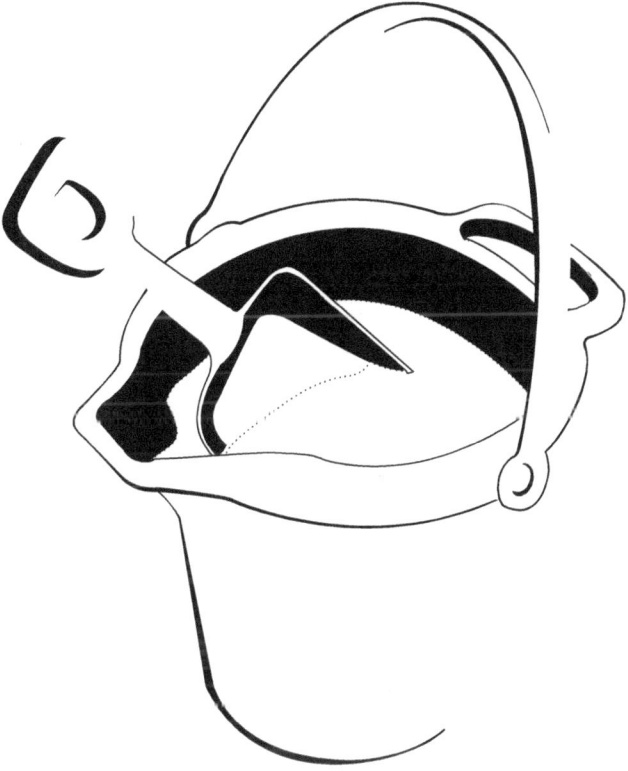

Light Source
The sand pail and shovel appear to be sitting in bright glaring sunlight as if at a beach. The use of extreme light and dark and closure enhance the feeling of light. The inventive handle is formed by two elliptical lines moving in opposite directions.

Telephone

Felicia Koloc

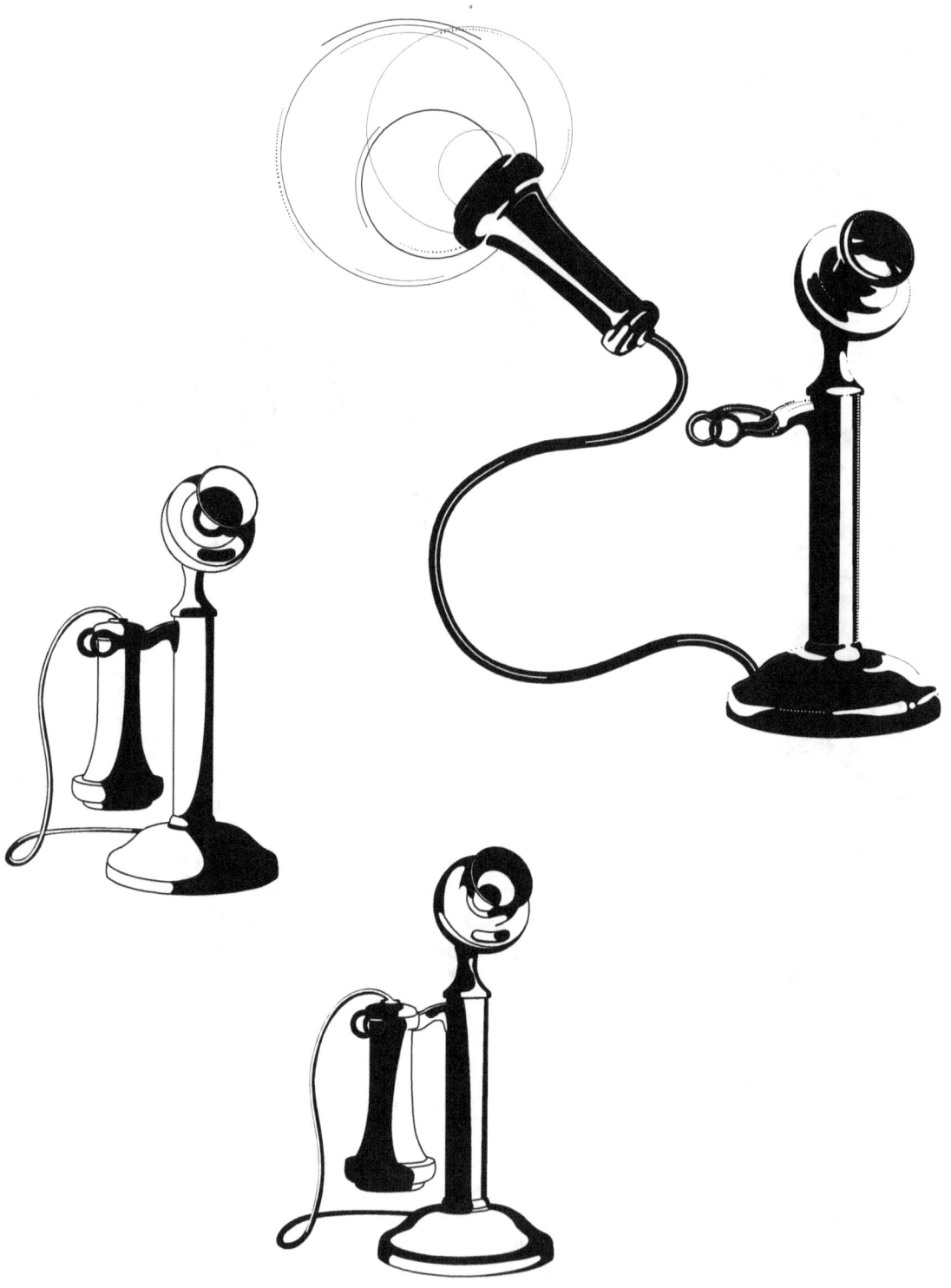

Telephone
Felicia Koloc

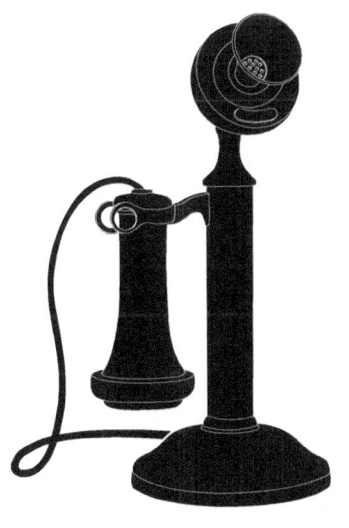

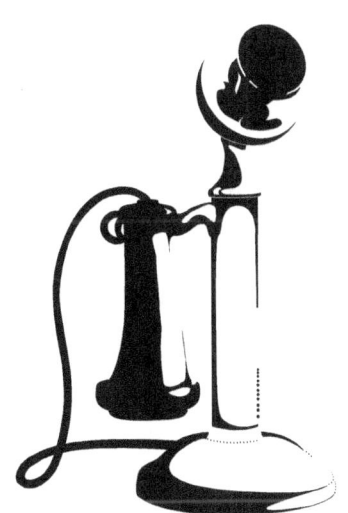

Exploratory hand-graphic drawing series.

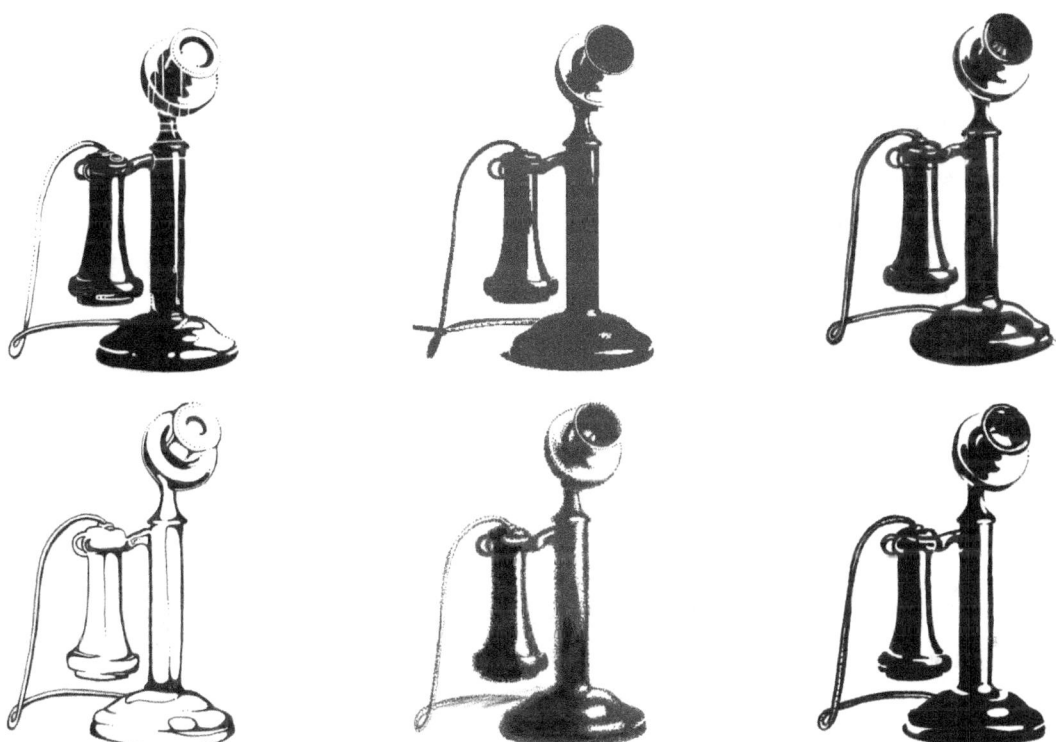

Swiss Army Knife
Christopher Roeleveld

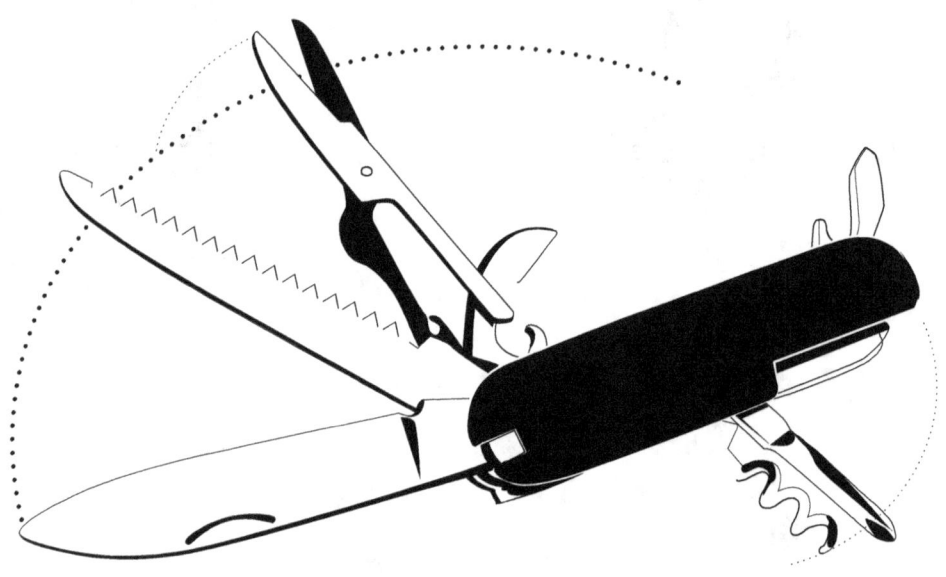

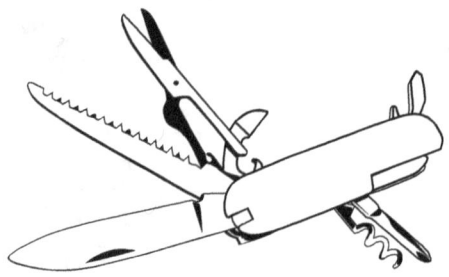

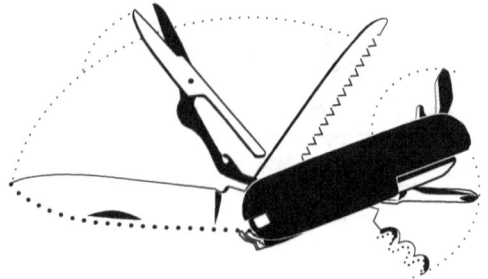

Swiss Army Knife

Christopher Roeleveld

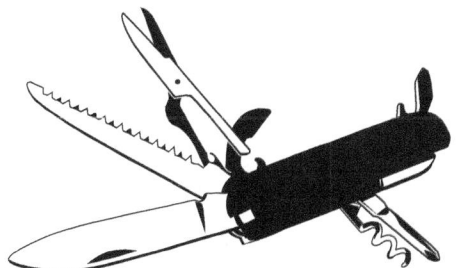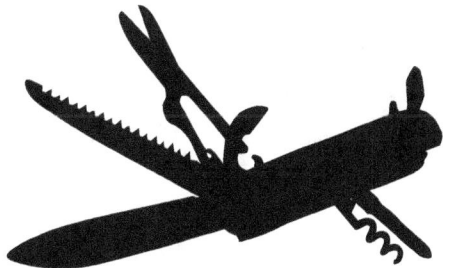

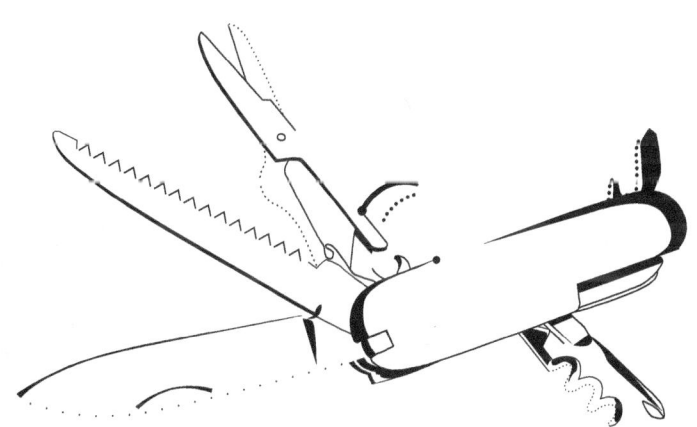

Sail Boat 2
Yael Rotstein

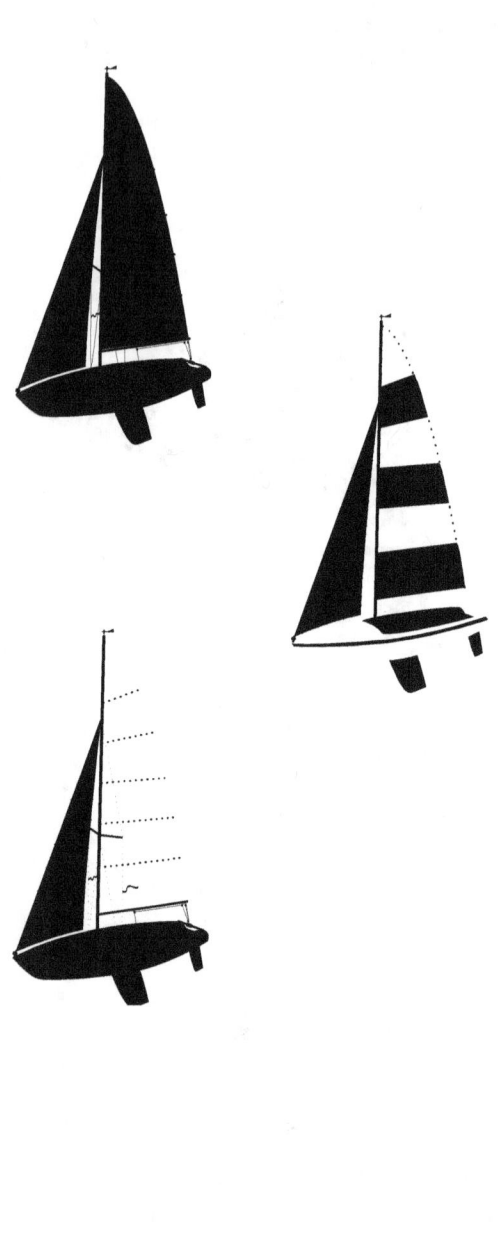

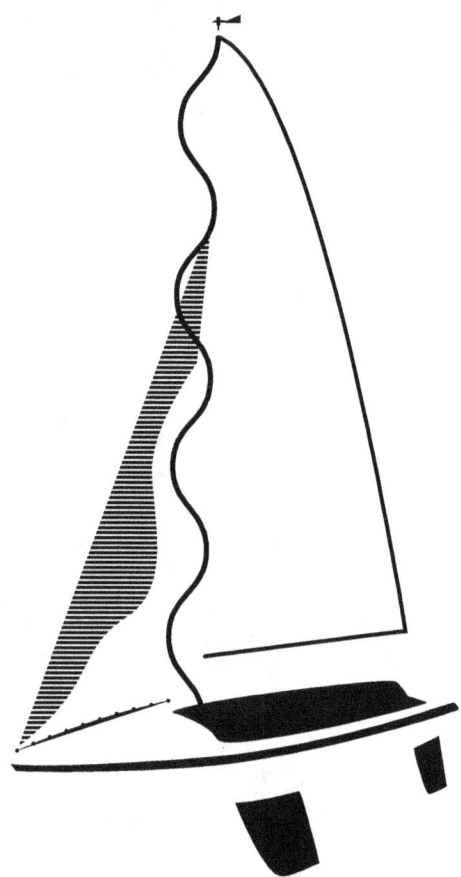

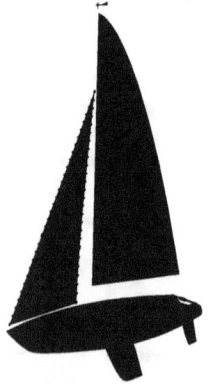

Sandal
Elaine Fong

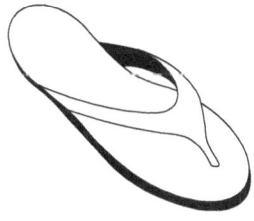

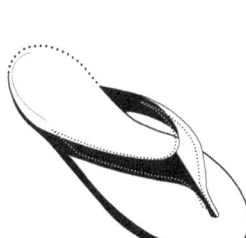

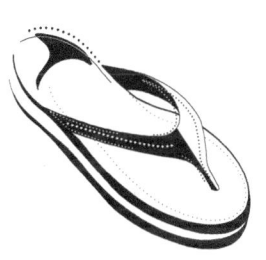

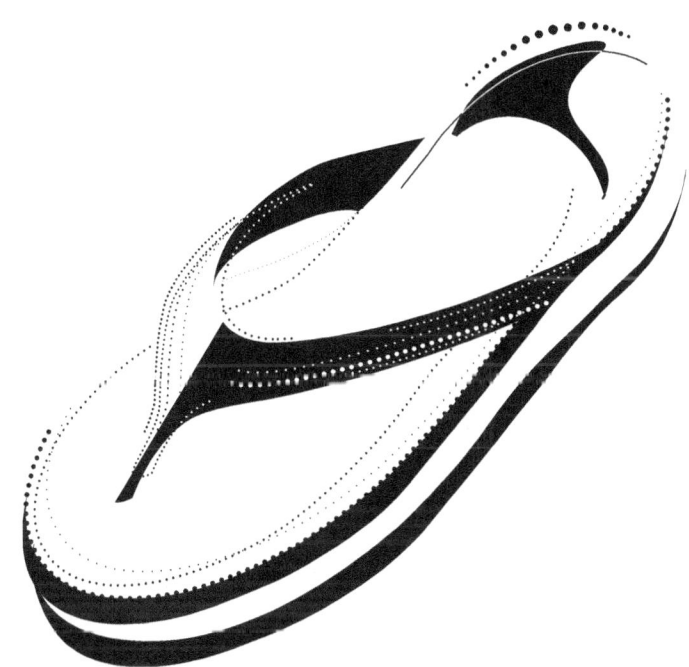

The Dotted Line
The creative use of the dotted line makes this ordinary beach sandal extraordinary. The dots repeat the movement of the "flip flop." Particularly interesting are the dots at the curve of the heel that change in size to enhance the movement of the eye around the form.

Scale

Amanda Clark

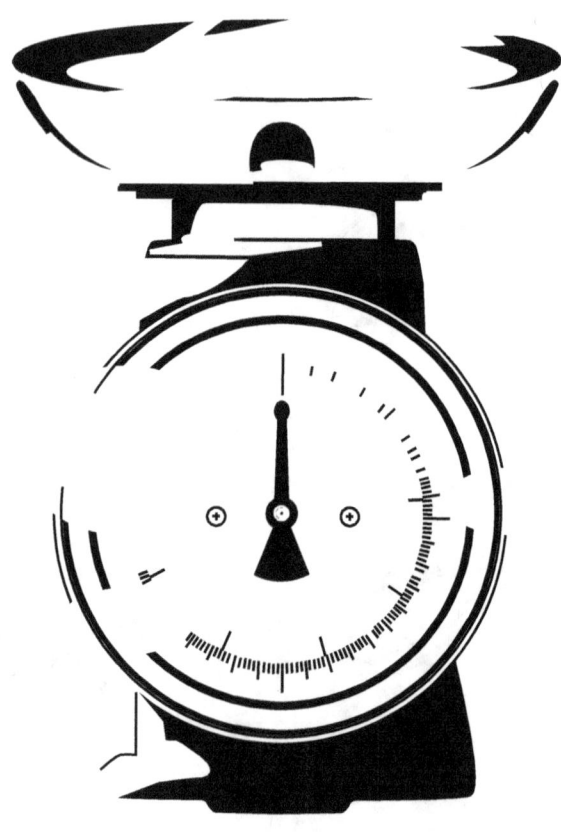

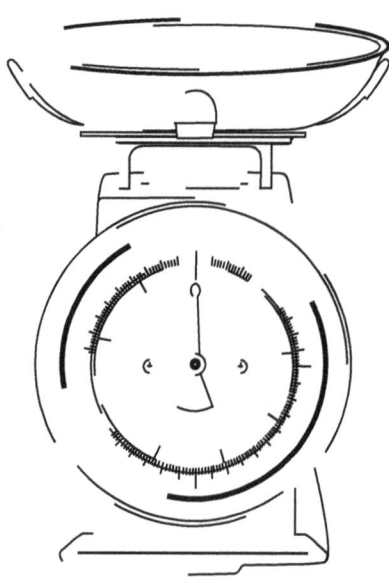

Scale

Amanda Clark

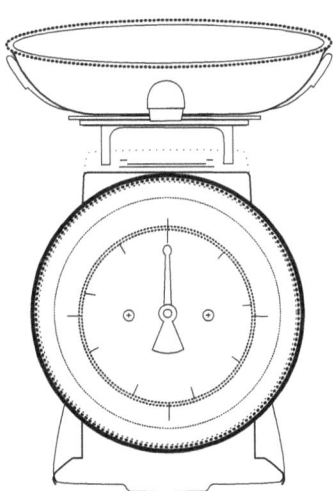

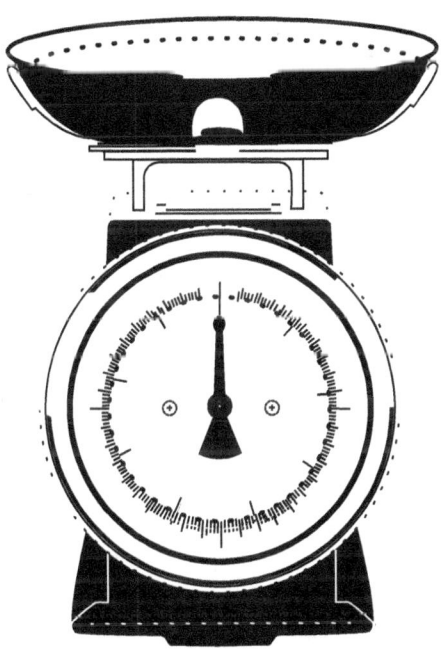

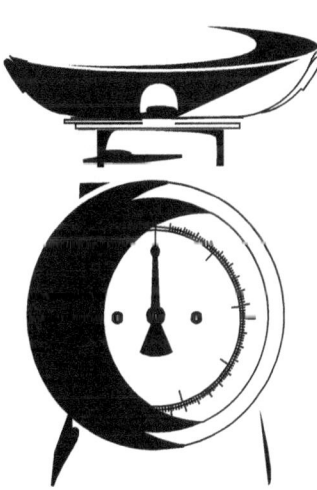

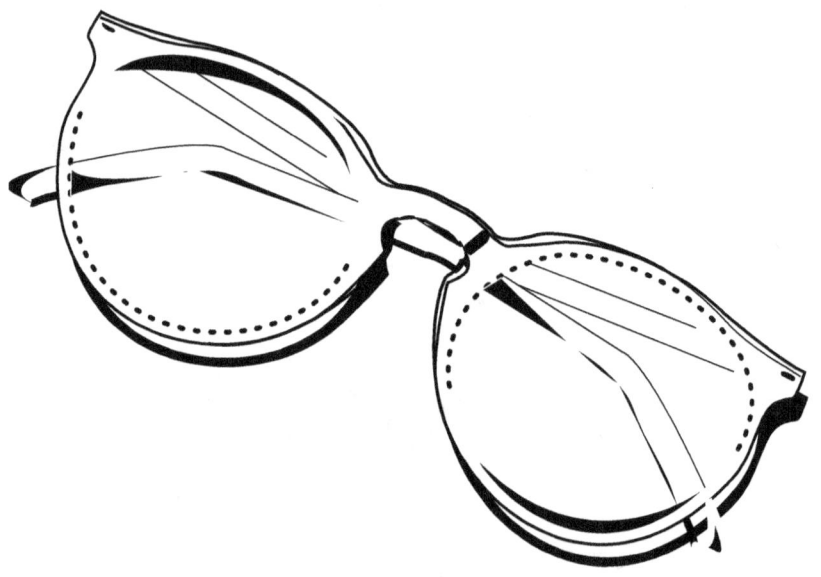

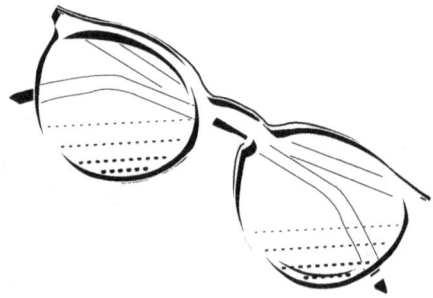

Sunglasses

Drew Chibbaro

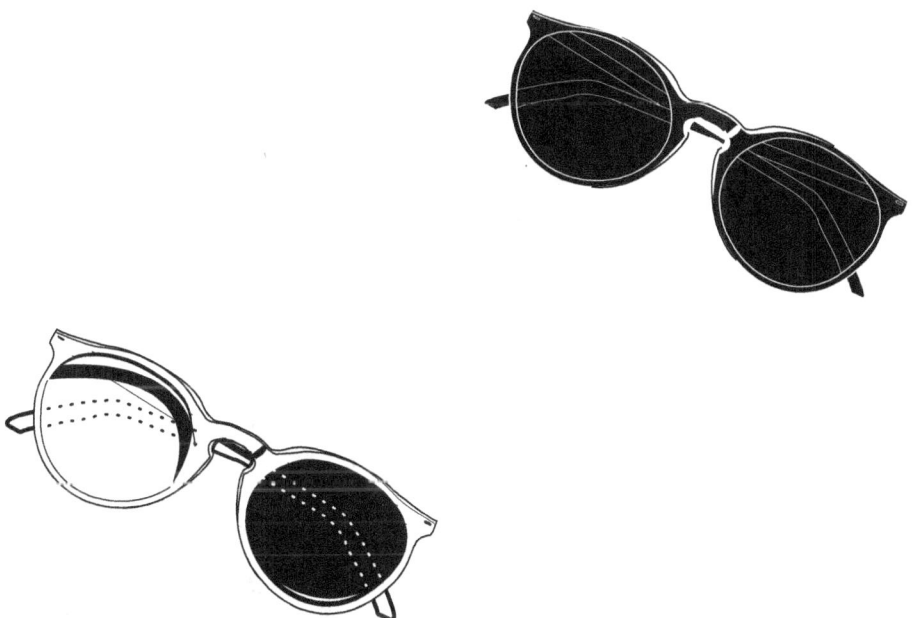

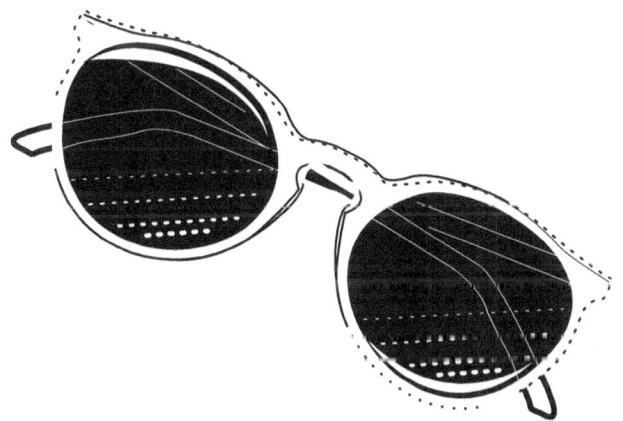

Toaster
Lenna Dahlquist

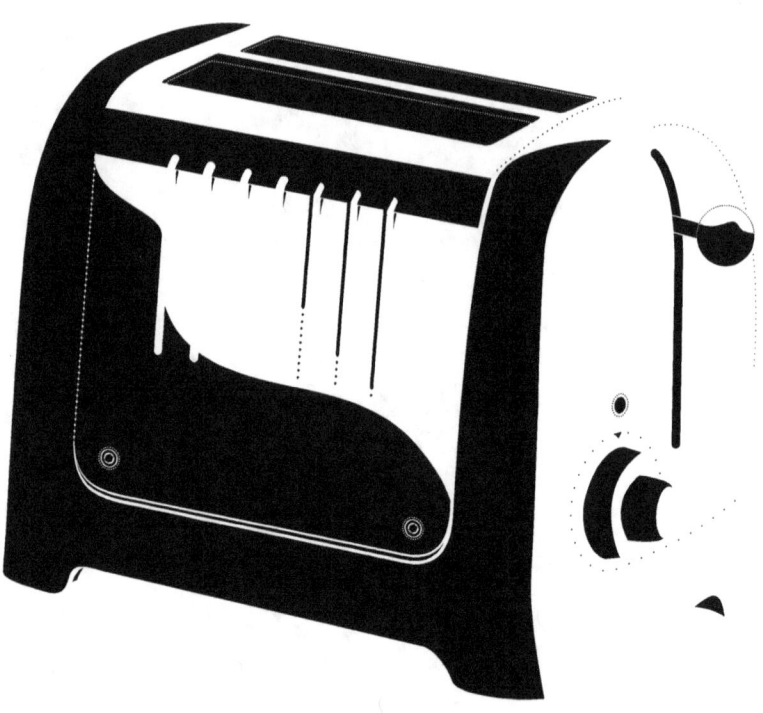

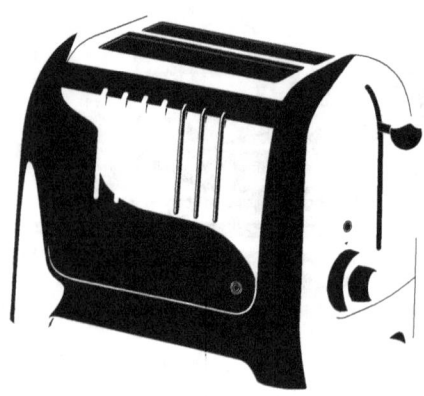

Toaster

Lenna Dahlquist

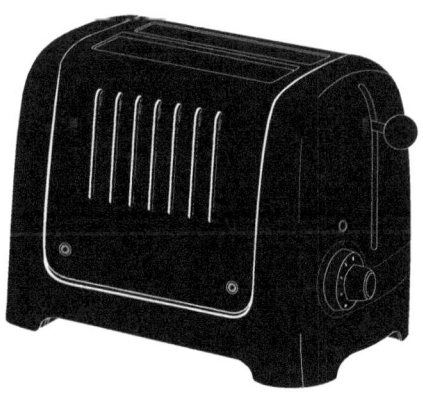

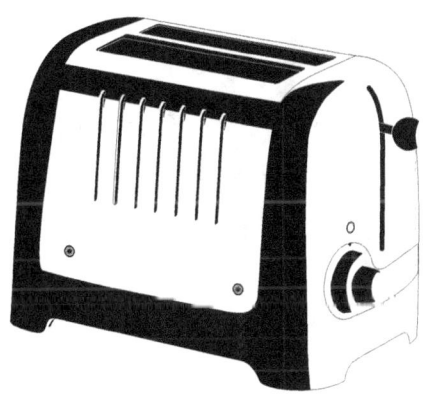

Exploratory hand-graphic drawing series.

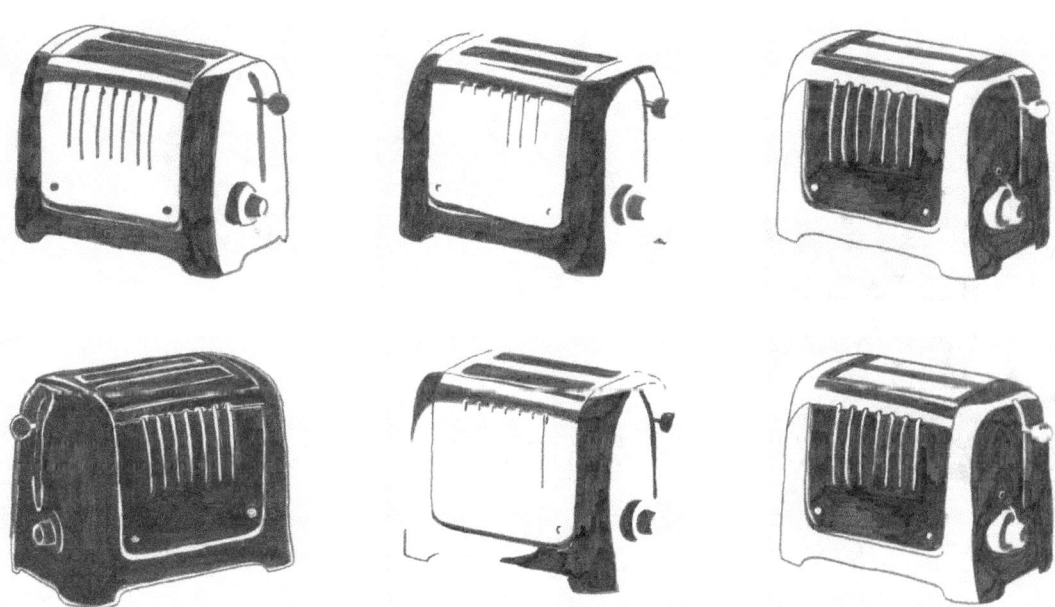

Umbrella 1

Yael Rotstein

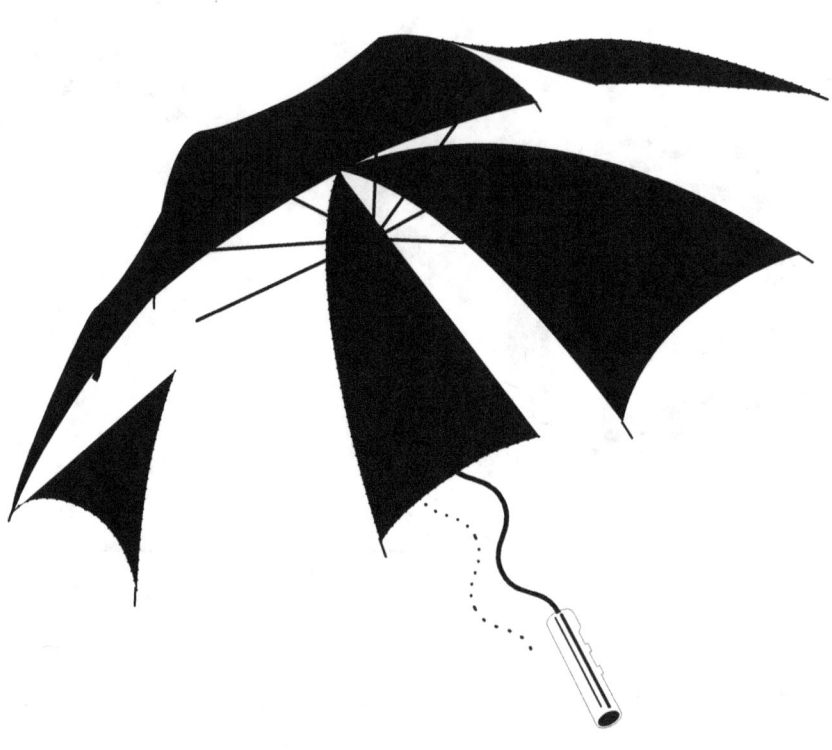

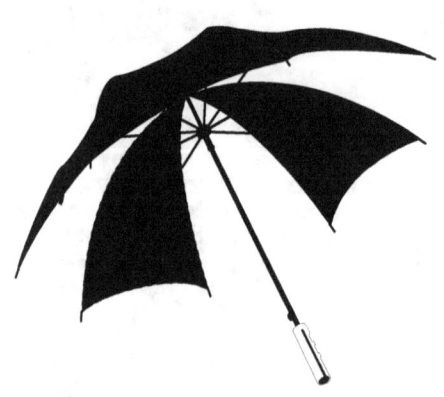

Umbrella 1

Yael Rotstein

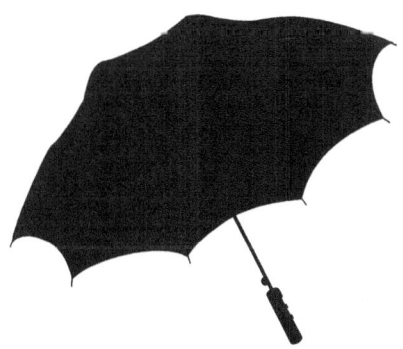

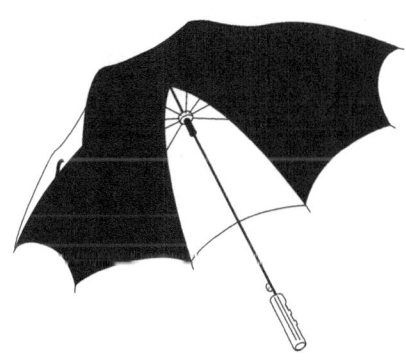

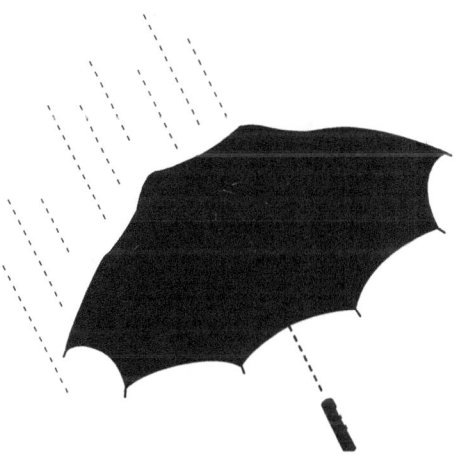

Umbrella 2
Tommy Bradley

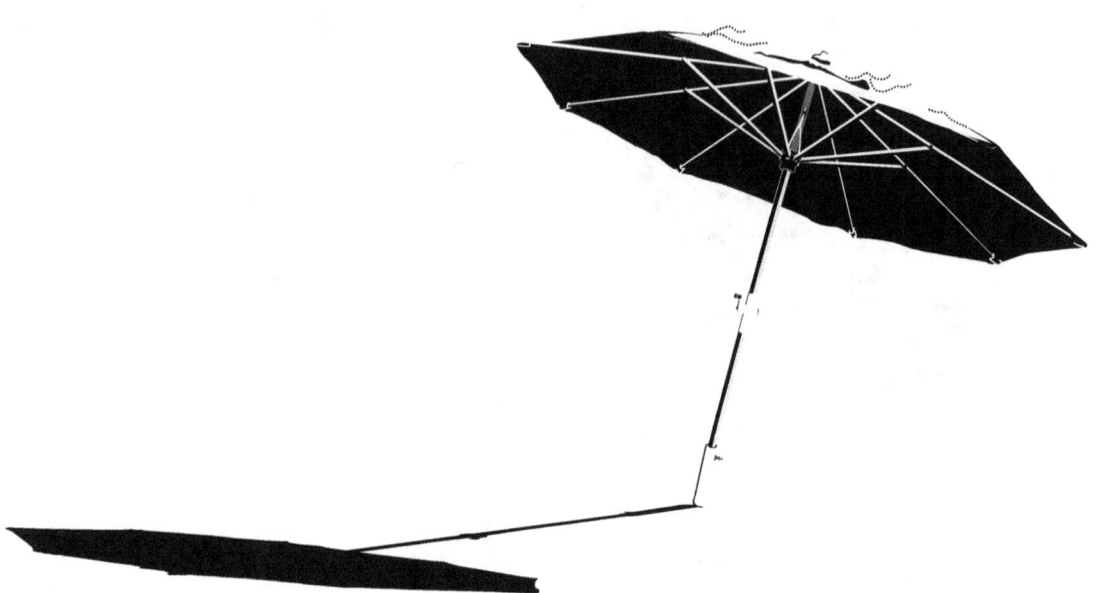

Umbrella 2

Tommy Bradley

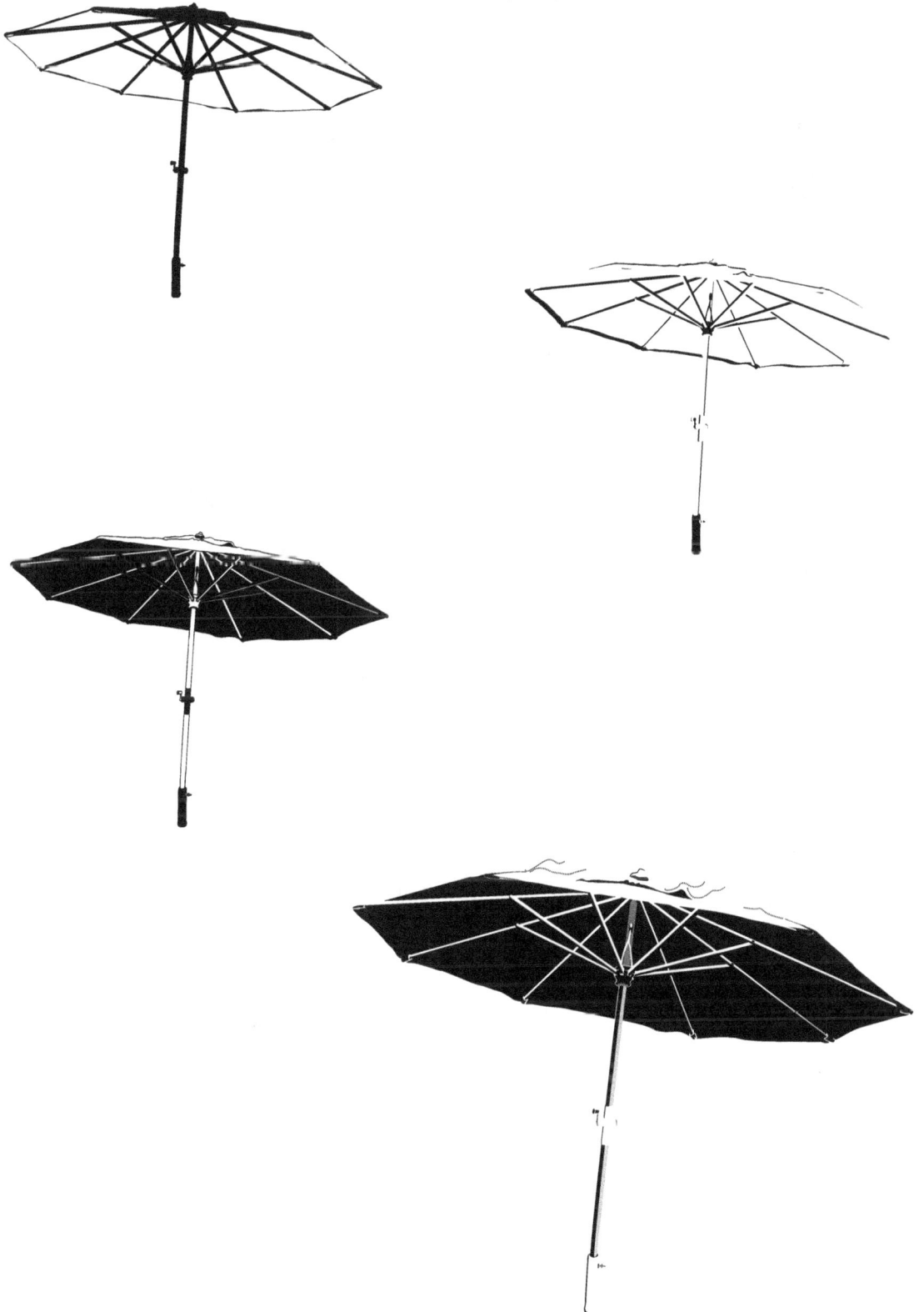

Umbrella 3

Brian Mah

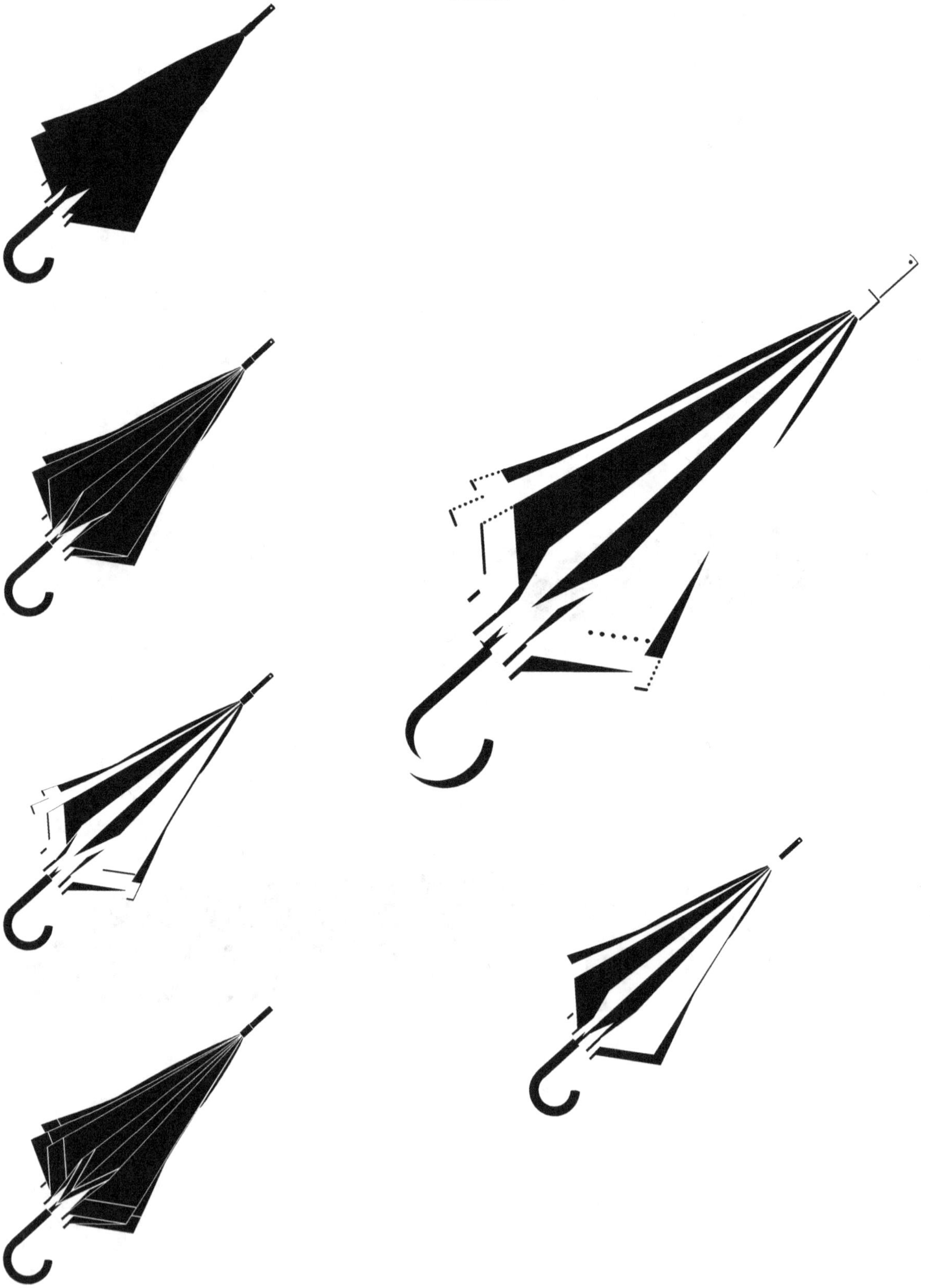

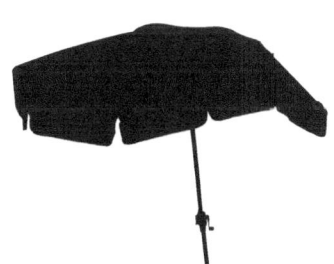

Umbrella 4
Sarah Petti

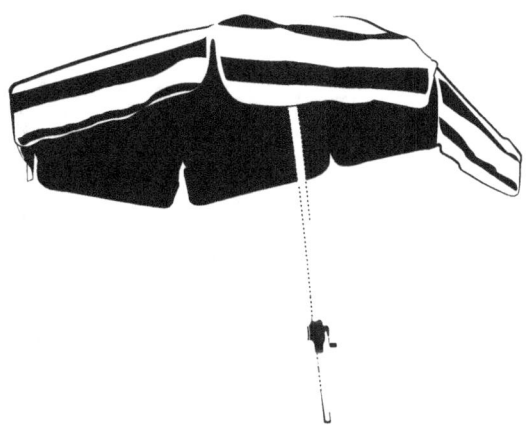

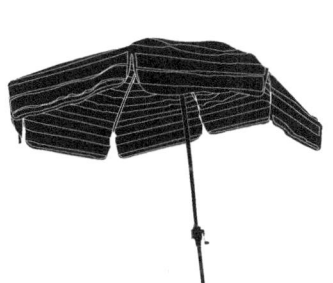

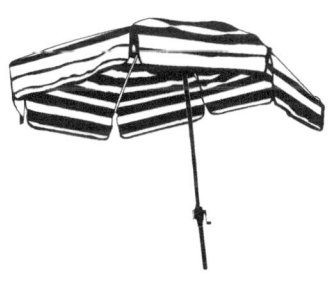

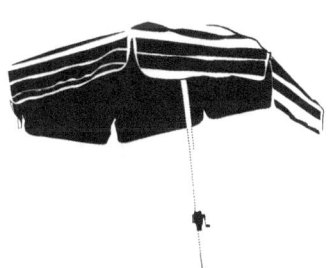

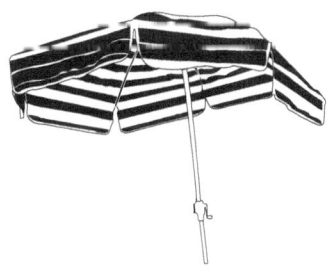

Vacuum
Camay Ho

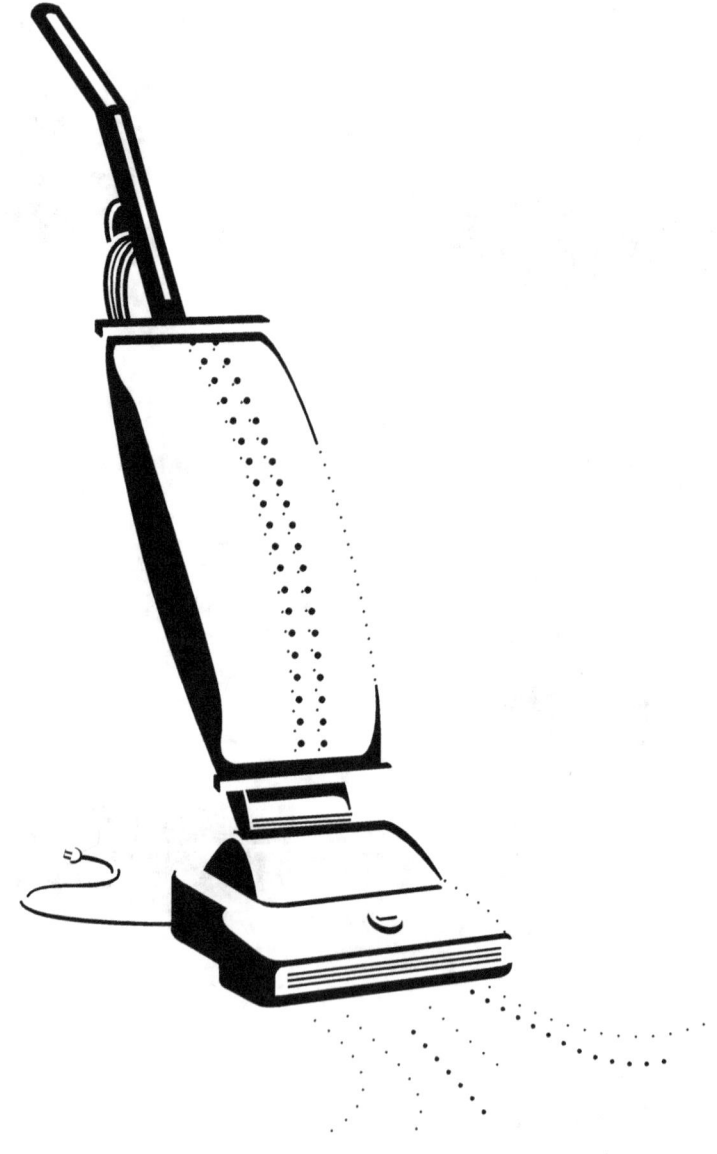

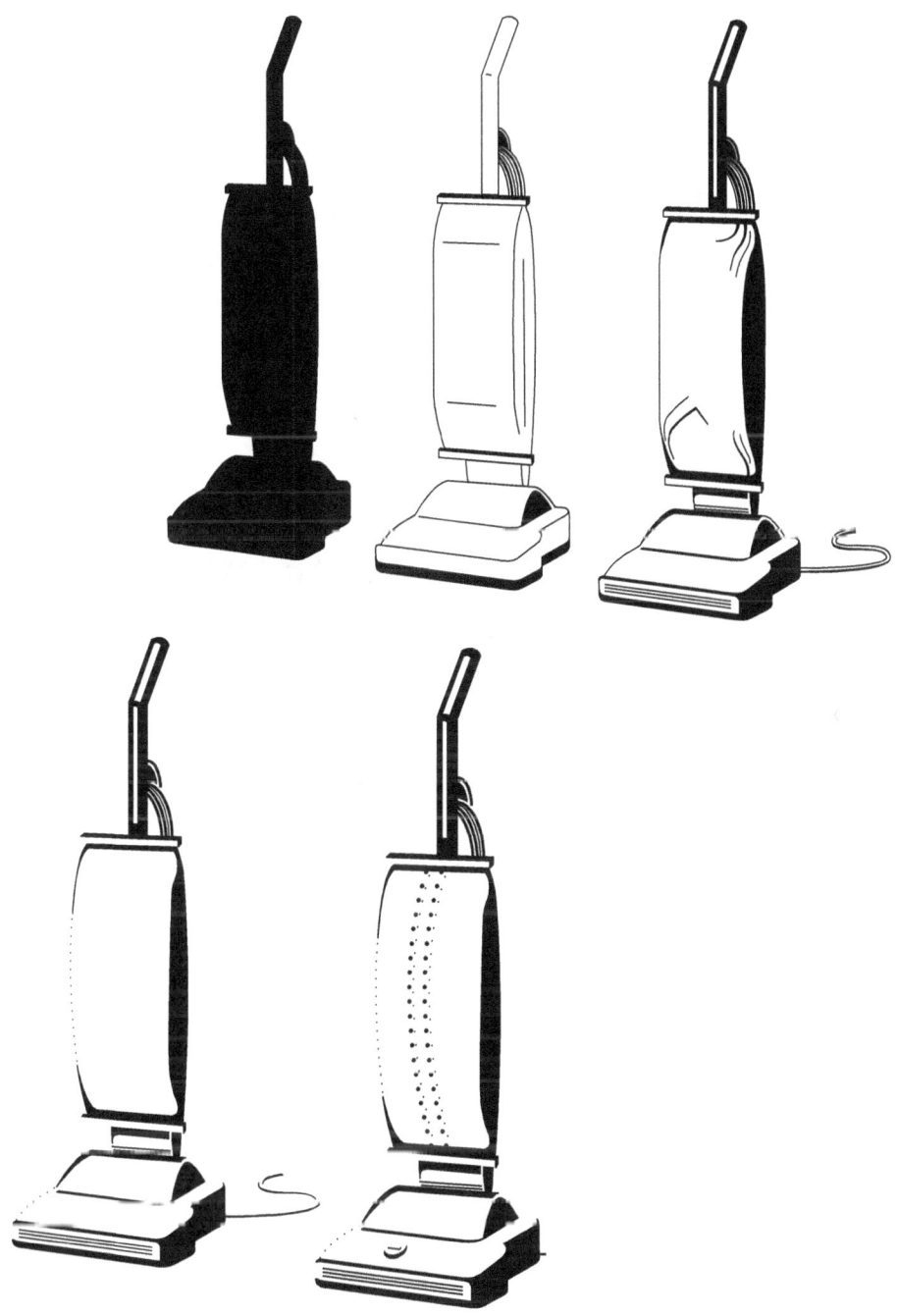

Wheelbarrow

Melissa Pena

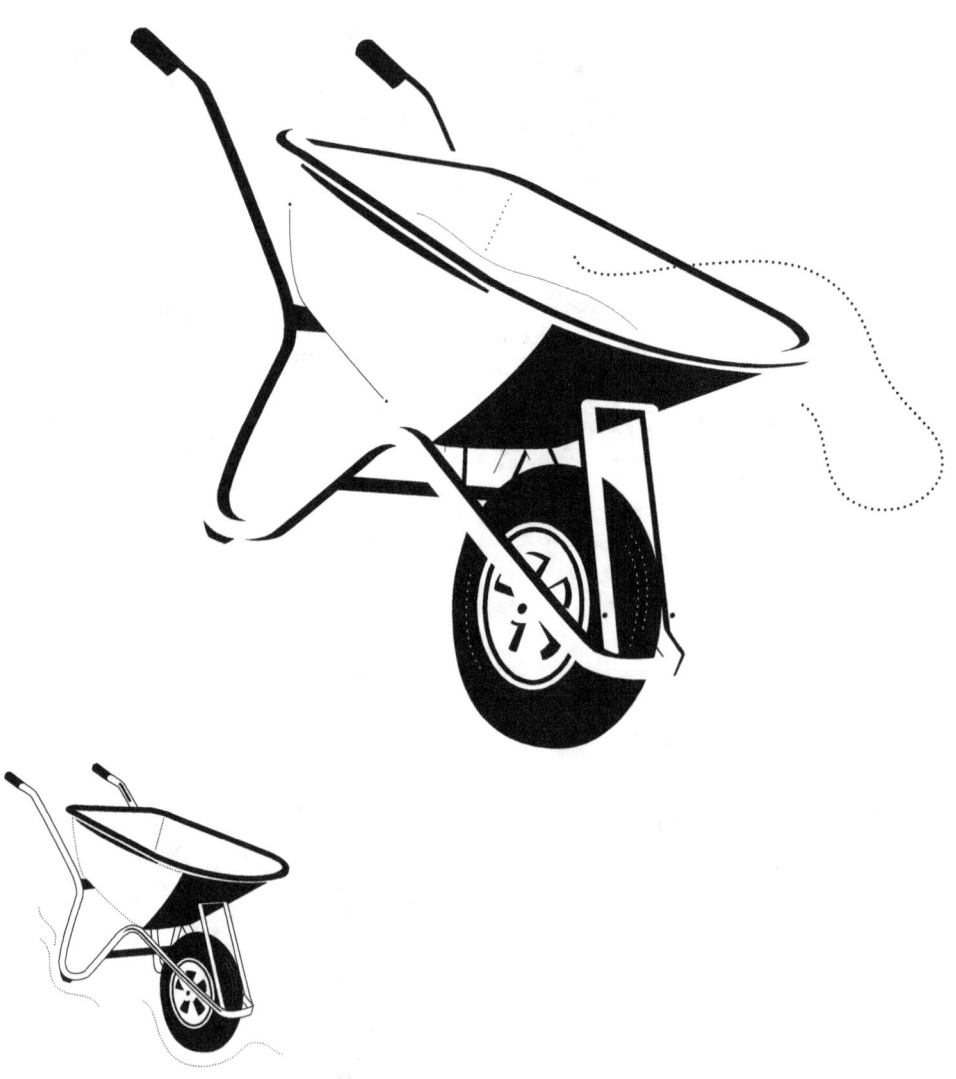

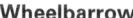

Wheelbarrow

Melissa Pena

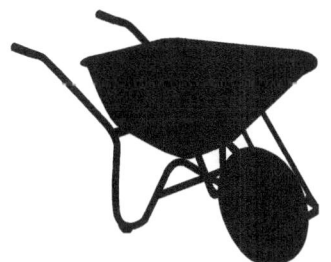

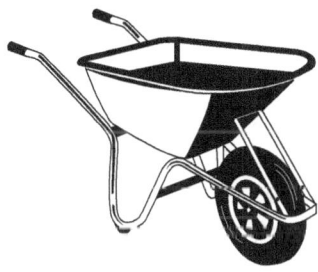

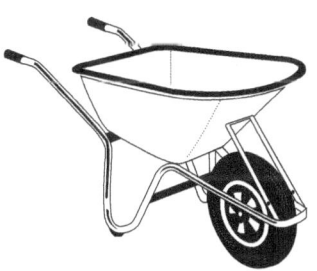

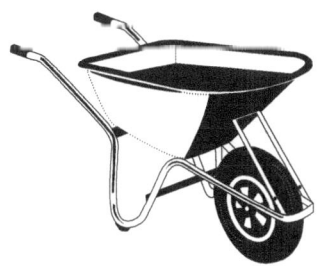

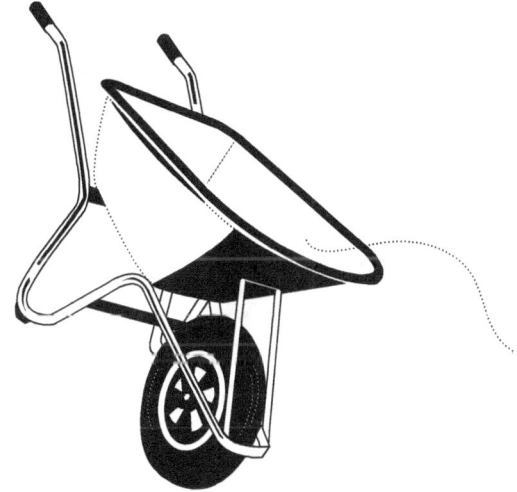

Whisk
Omar Mendez

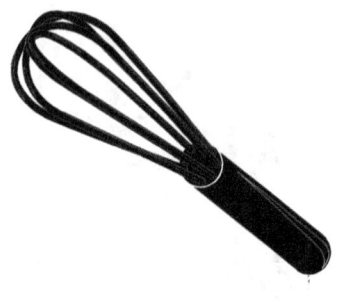

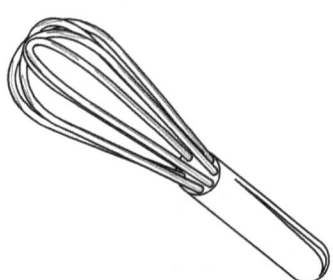

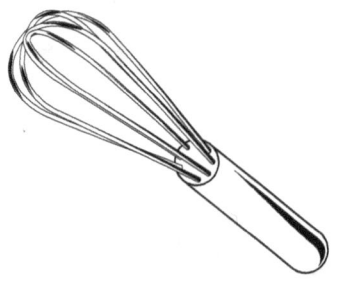

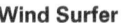

Wind Surfer

Sarah Petti

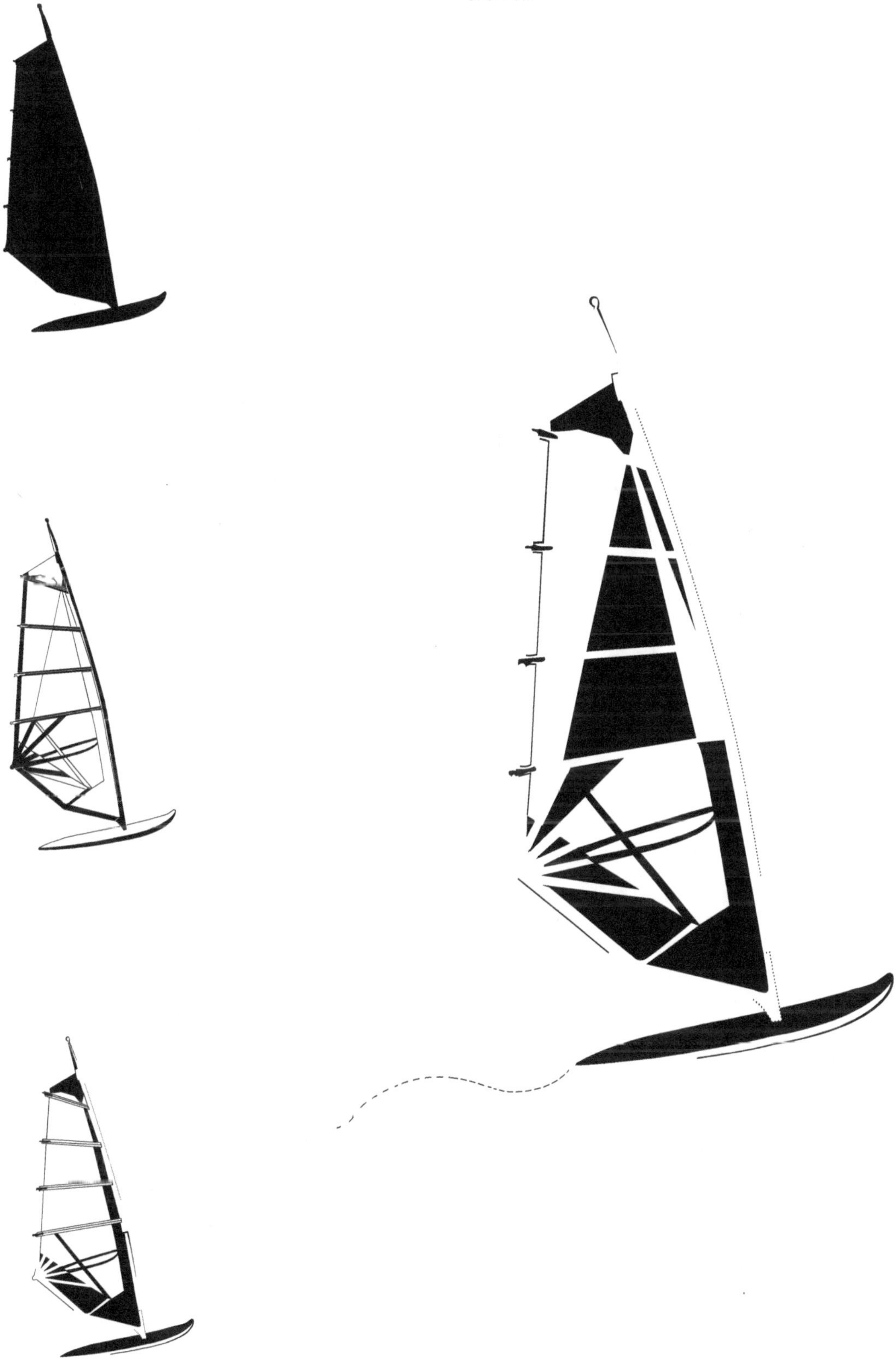

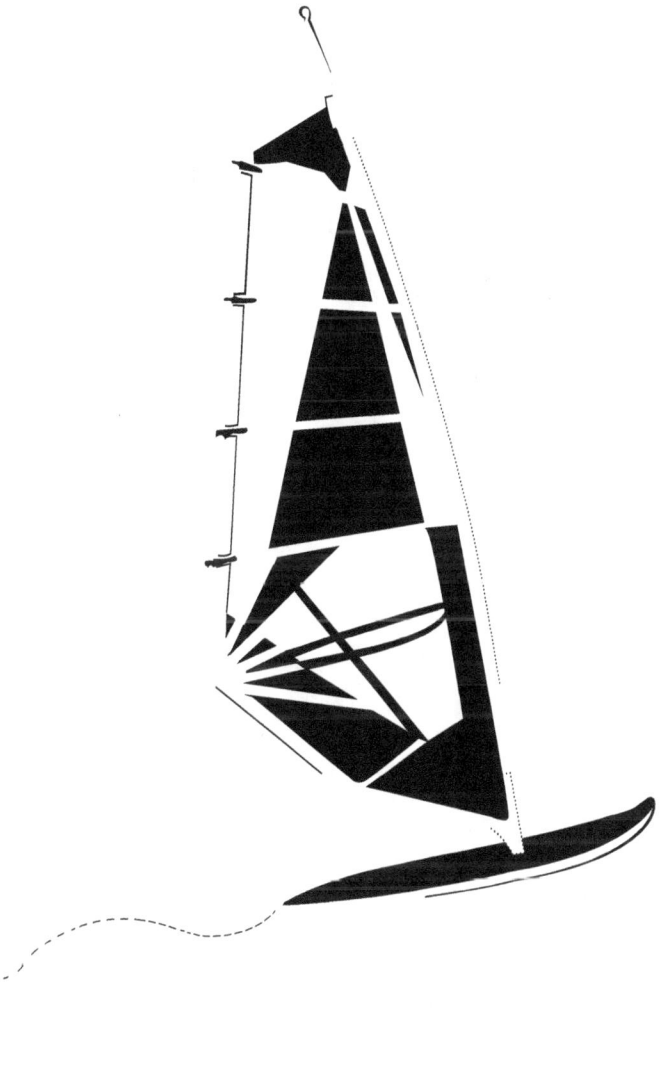

Miscellaneous

These works are shown as individuals because
only the final step was archived. Although the
steps in the process are missing the final results
are satisfying.

Shell 1
Brian Mah

Shell 2
Katherine Mickey

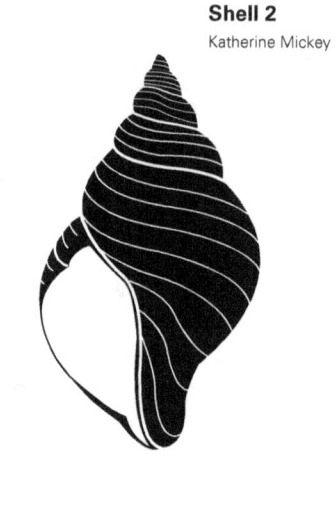

Shell 3
Elaine Fong

Shell 4
Amy Leet

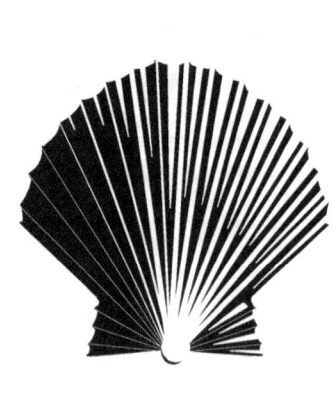

Miscellaneous

Frog 1
Scott Tennant

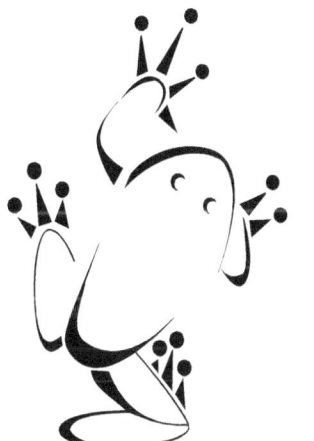

Mosquito
Scott Tennant

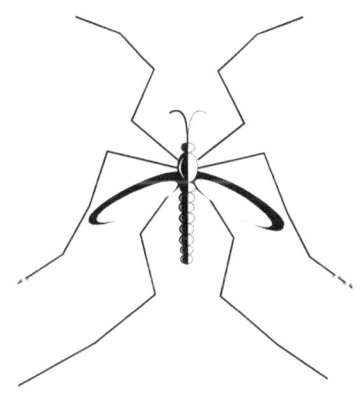

Ladybug 1
Laura Bucklew

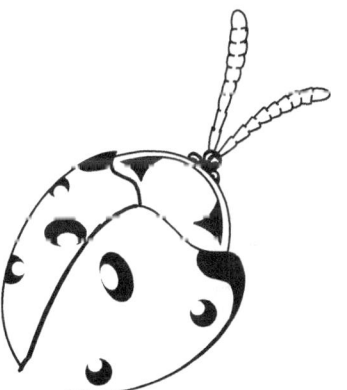

Crab
Michelle Jablonski

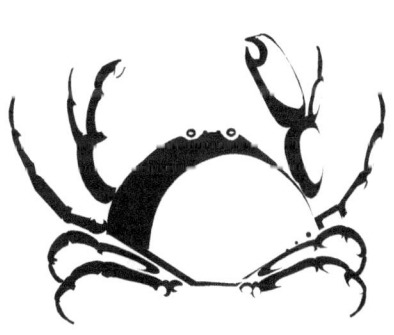

Palm 1

Katherine Mickey

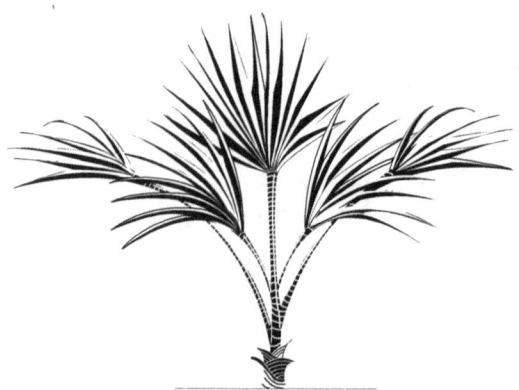

Banana Tree

Amy Leet

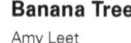

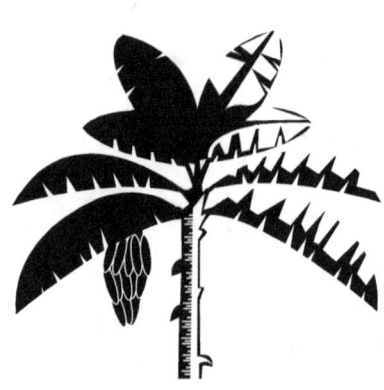

Palm 2

Scott Hay

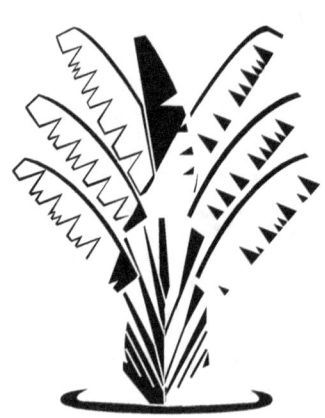

Pineapple

Theresa Eichten

Miscellaneous

Water Bottle
Brian Mah

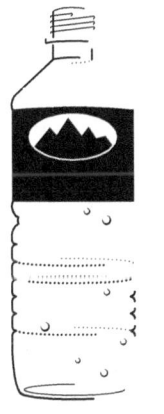

Seagull 1
Sarah Irani

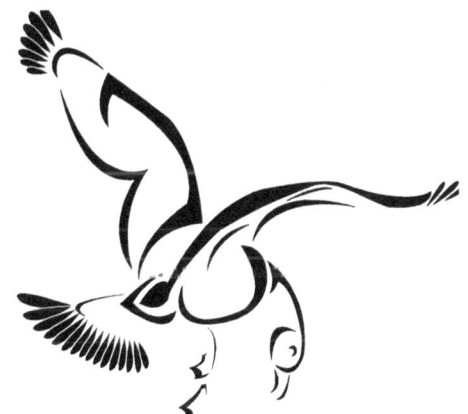

Tuna
Jason Richardson

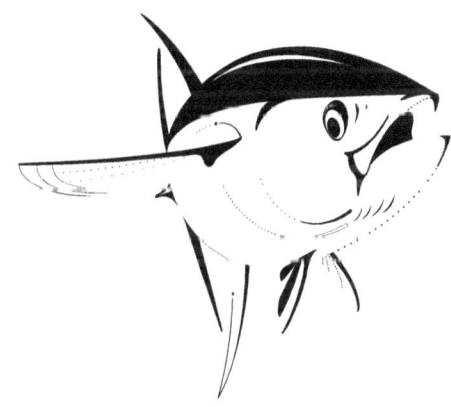

Rollerblade
Jana Dee Bassingthwaite

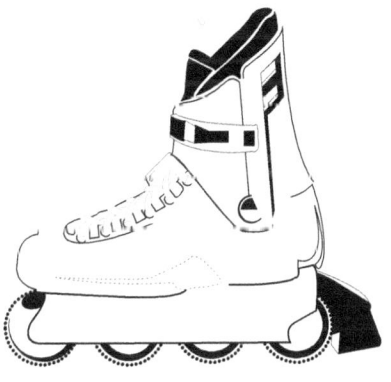

Alligator 1
Annie Riker

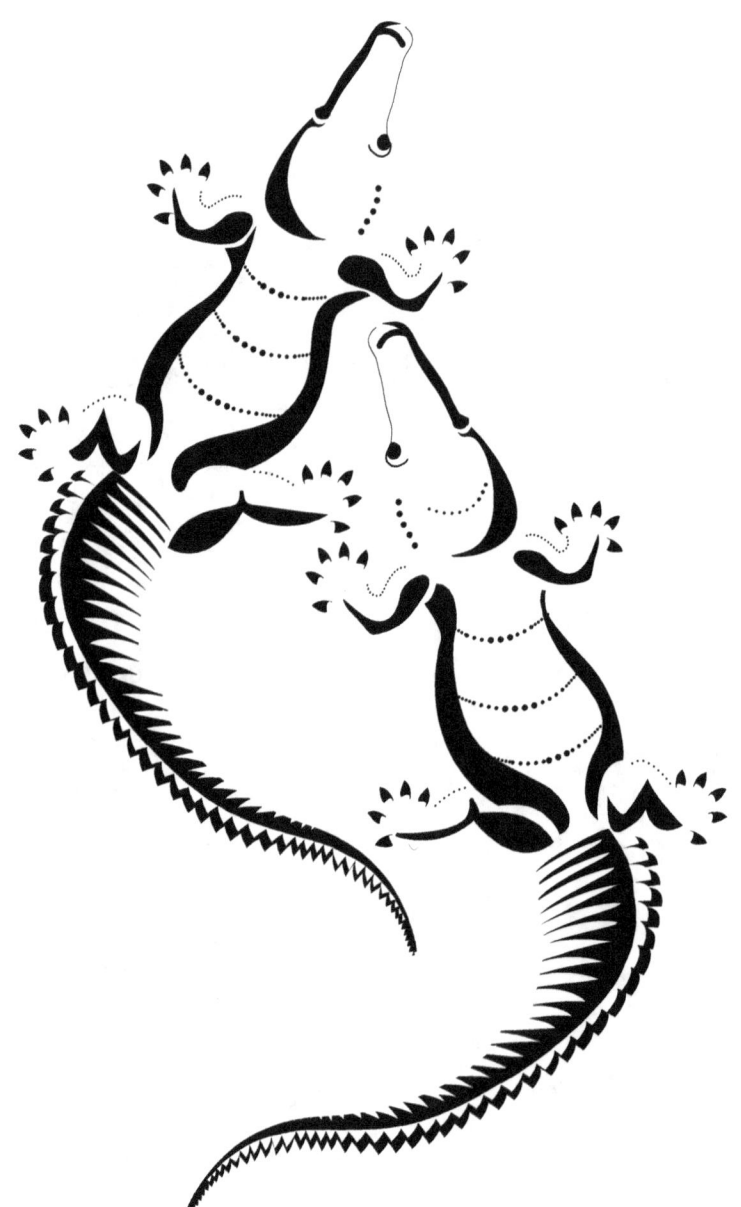

Repetition of Object
Grouping of two alligators rather than just one
emphasizes the curvilinear forms. The graceful
tails employ a repetition of similar shapes and the
negative space between the alligators becomes
part of the drawing.

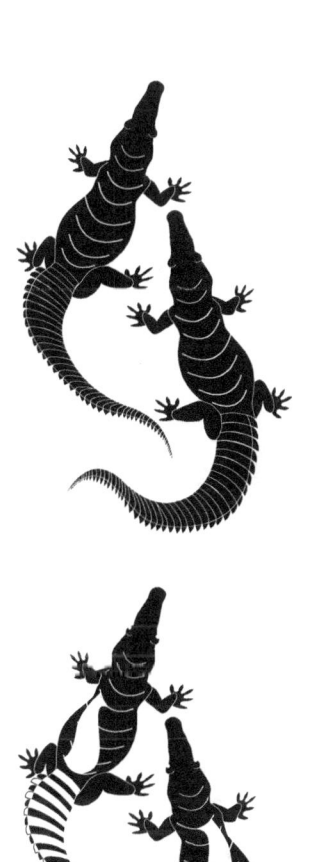

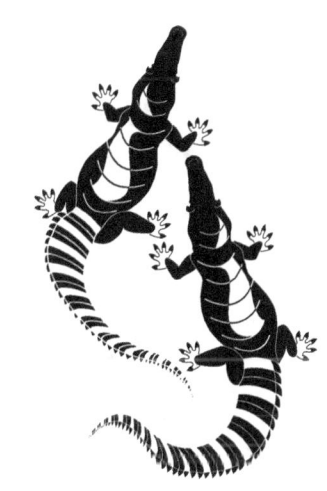

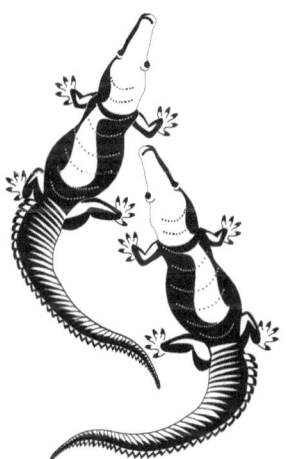

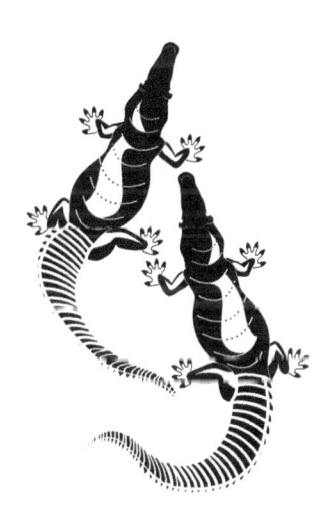

Alligator 2
Ronnie Koff

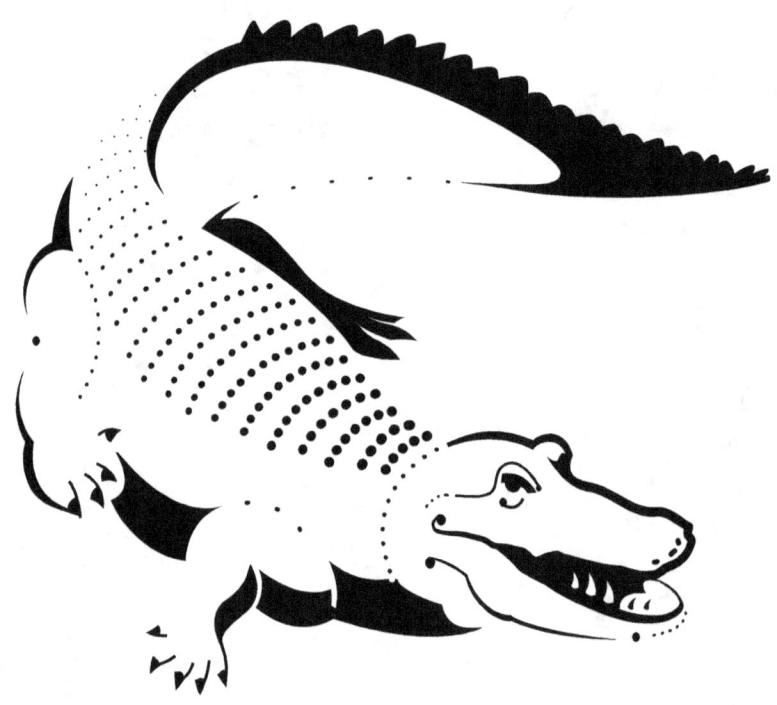

Texture Repetition
Rhythm and repetition of texture make this drawing
come to life. The eye follows the repeated bumps
on the tail to the texture on the back. The eye is
further guided by a repeated dot texture as the dots
gradually become larger.

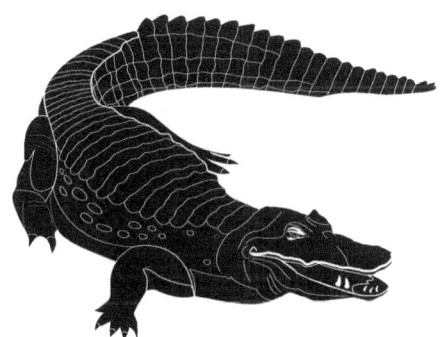

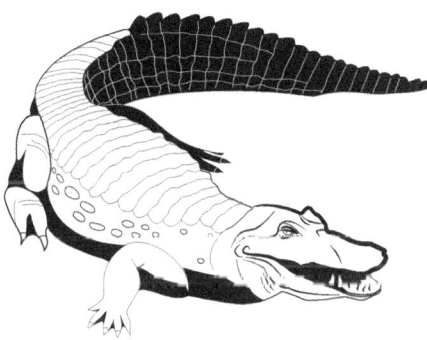

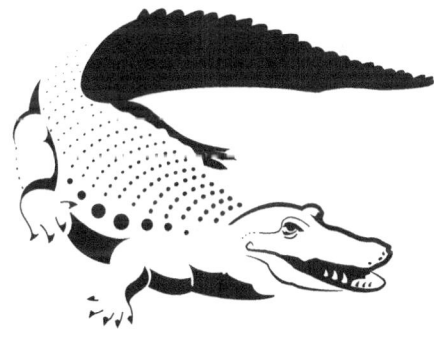

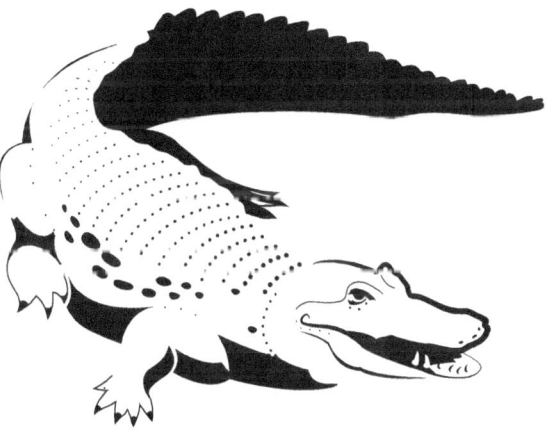

Bee

Loni Diep

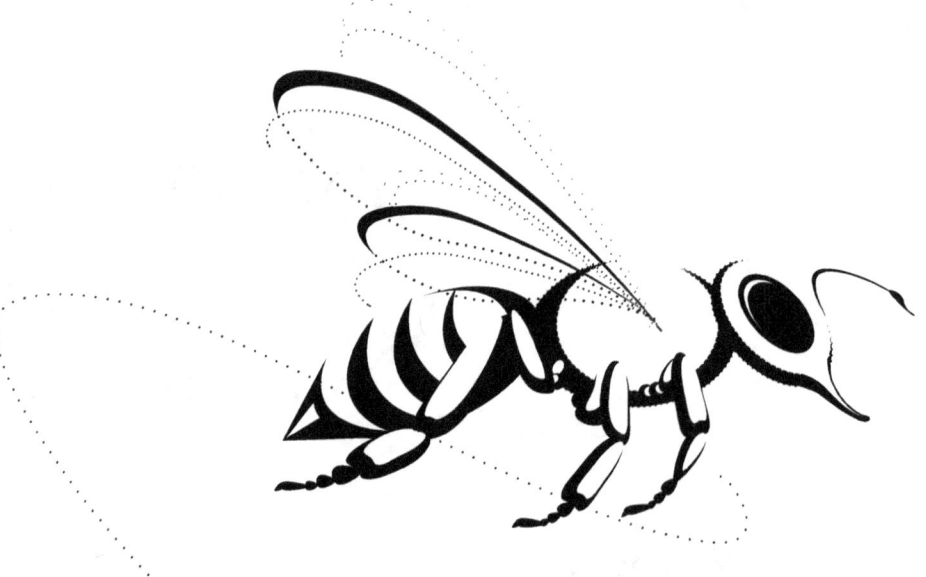

Harmony of Shape

The balance of dark and light plus the use of exquisite shapes makes this drawing beautiful. The curvilinear pointed triangles that define the body are in harmony with the ellipse that is the eye. In the final phases of the translation the bees head was rotated up and the legs moved back to give it a feeling of movement in flight. The wings are transparent and are defined by repeated dotted and solid lines to give them motion.

Bee

Loni Diep

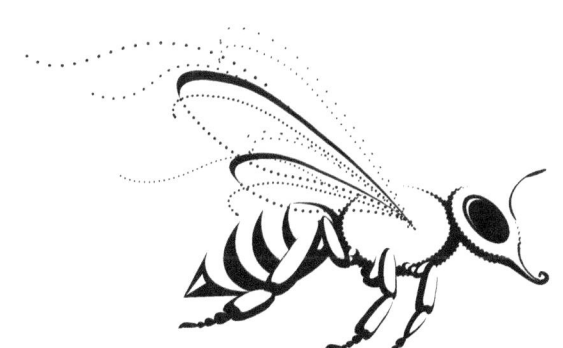

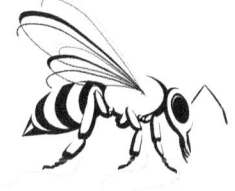

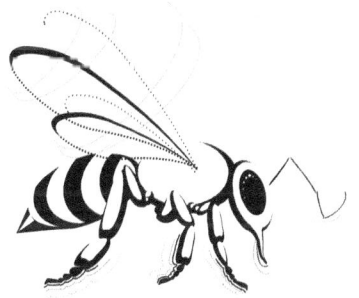

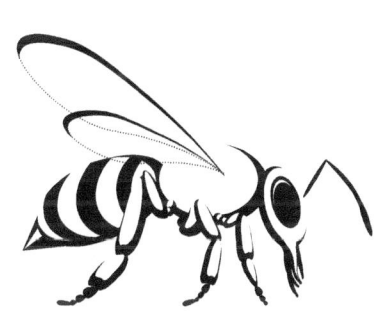

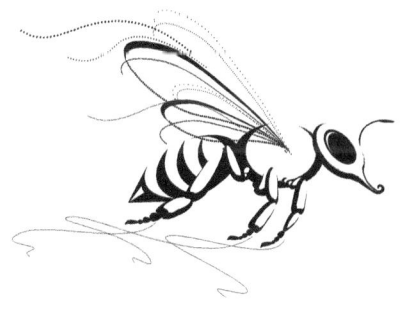

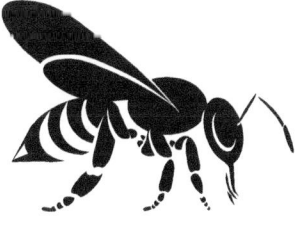

Beetle

Sarah Irani

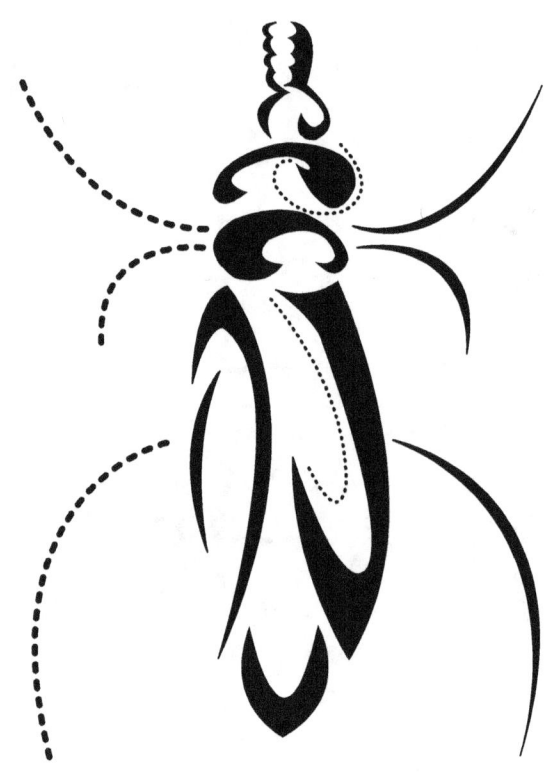

Beetle

Sarah Irani

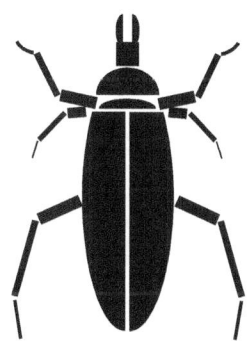

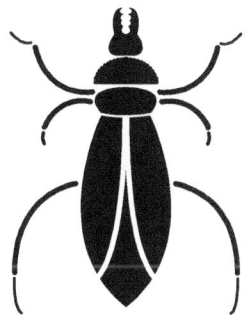

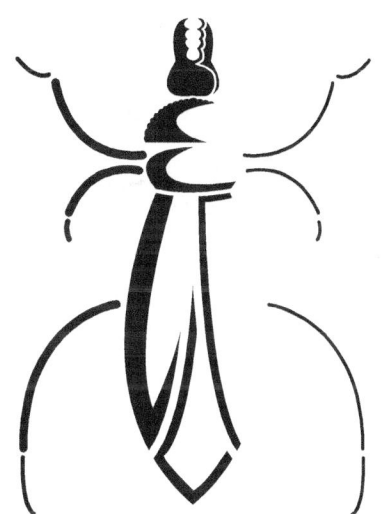

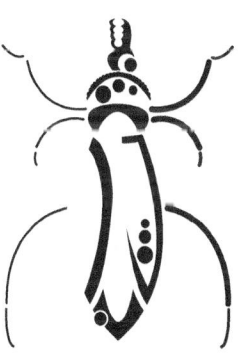

Butterfly

Heather Hickman

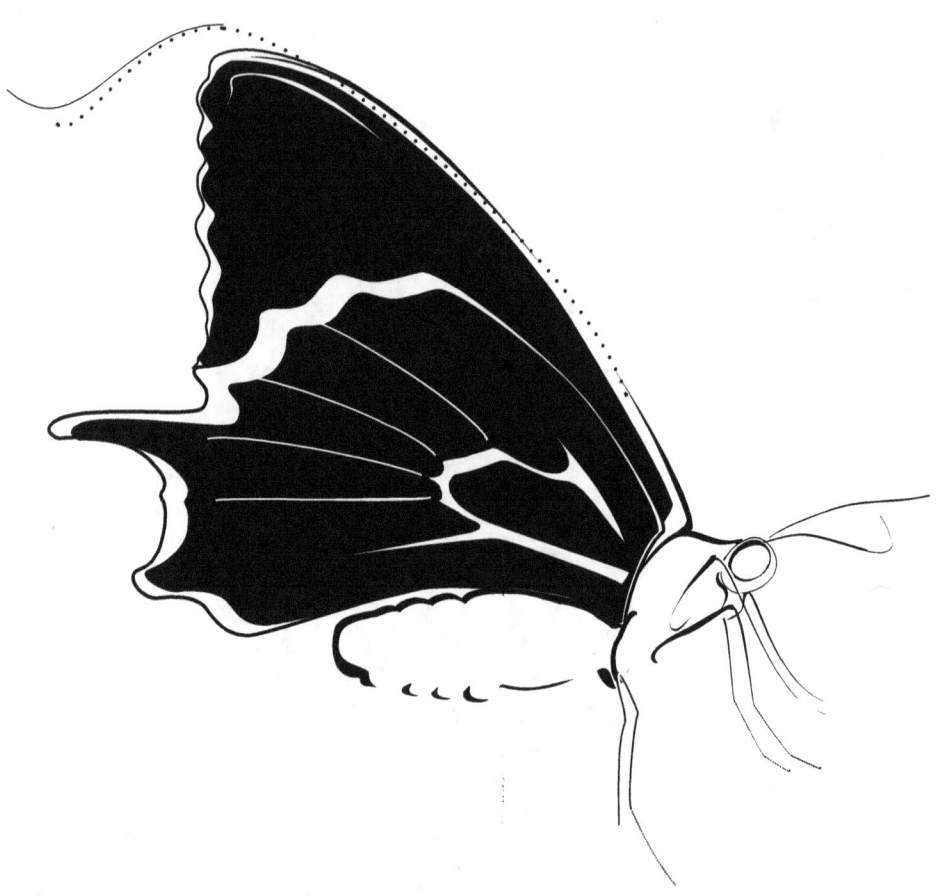

Butterfly
Heather Hickman

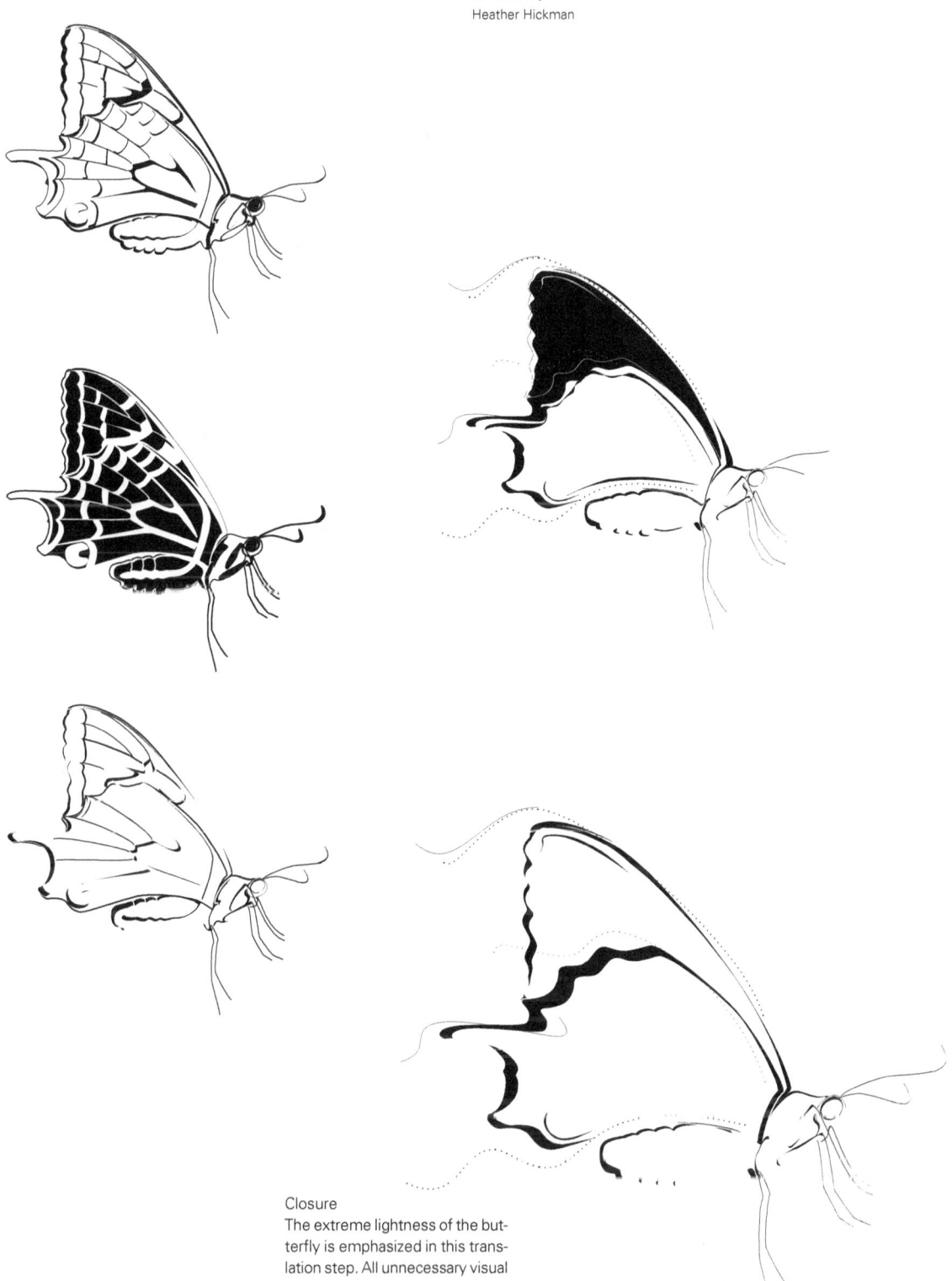

Closure
The extreme lightness of the butterfly is emphasized in this translation step. All unnecessary visual information is stripped away with just the minimum necessary for recognition.

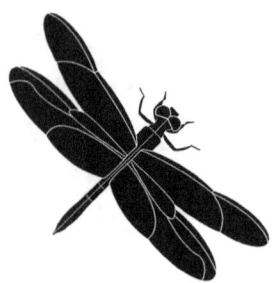

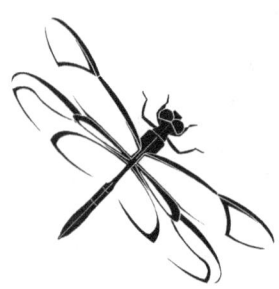

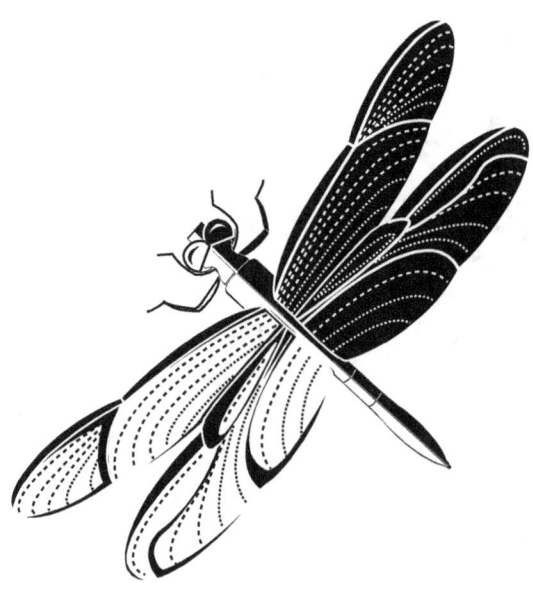

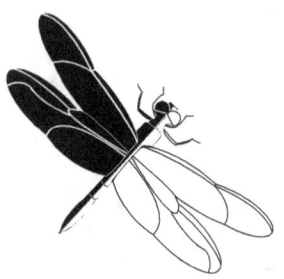

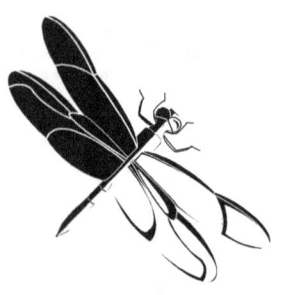

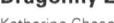

Dragonfly 2
Katherine Chase

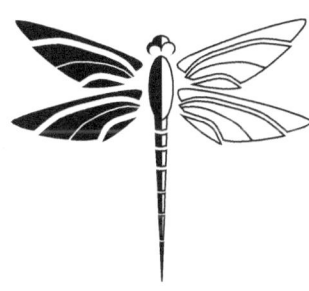

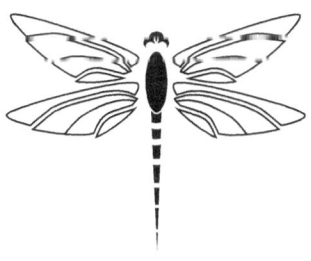

Egret
Ronnie Koff

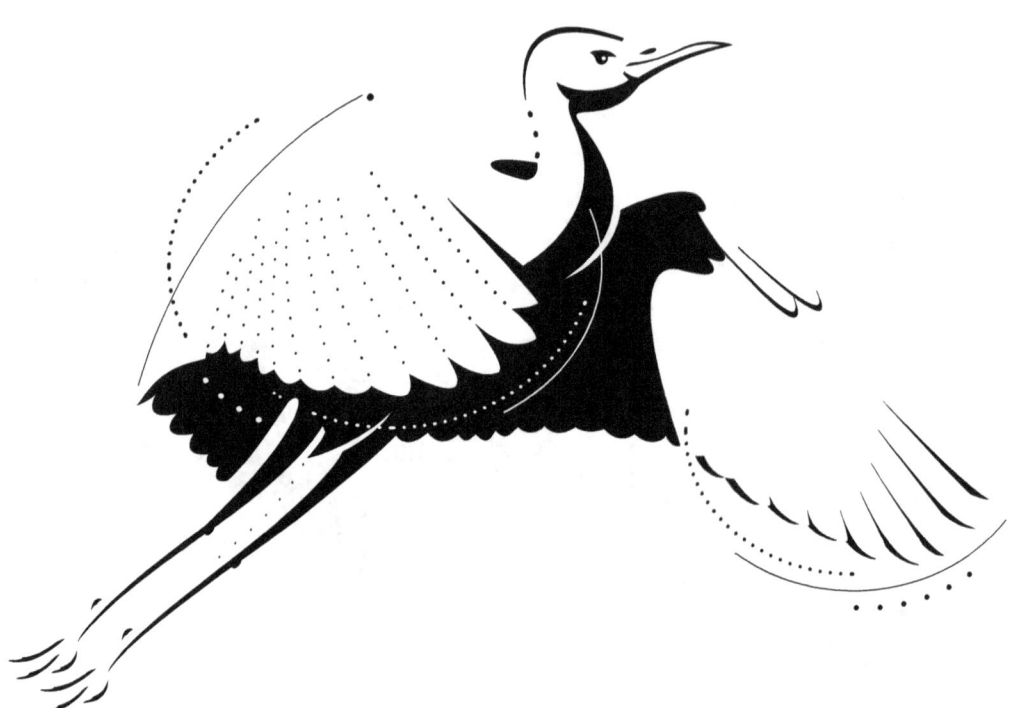

Elegance in Point, Line and Plane
The pose and the line work create an incredibly graceful egret. The wings are made with repeated feather shapes that are defined by dots on the top wing and lines on the bottom wing. In the final drawings of the series the beak of the egret is restyled, the top of the wing is defined with a line and single dot, and the illusion of flight is added. The variation in movement includes solid lines, tightly spaced dotted lines, and widely spaced dotted lines adds to the grace and beauty of the drawing.

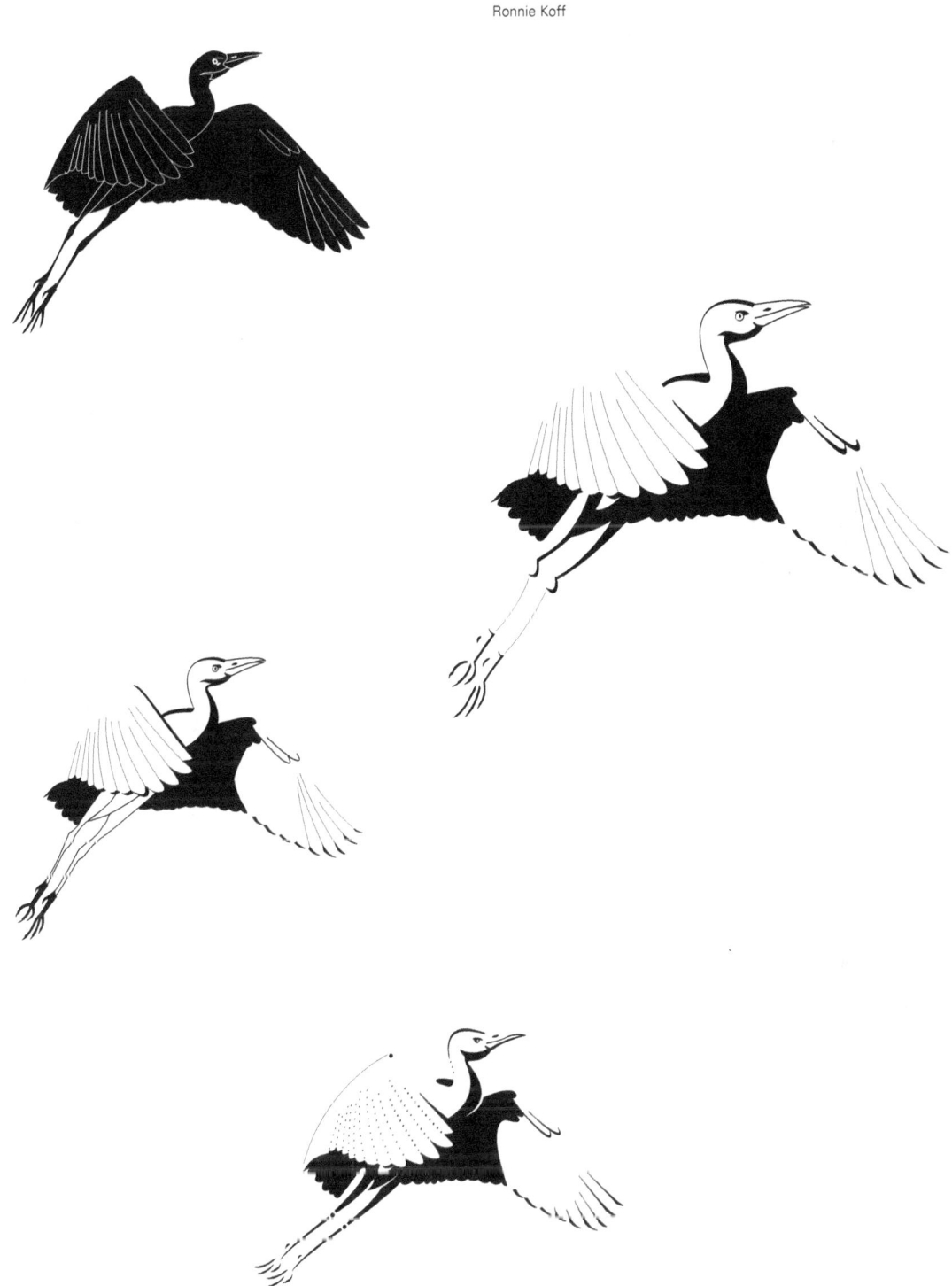

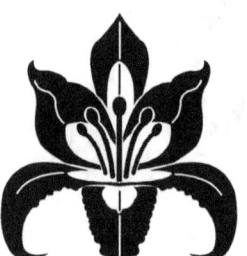

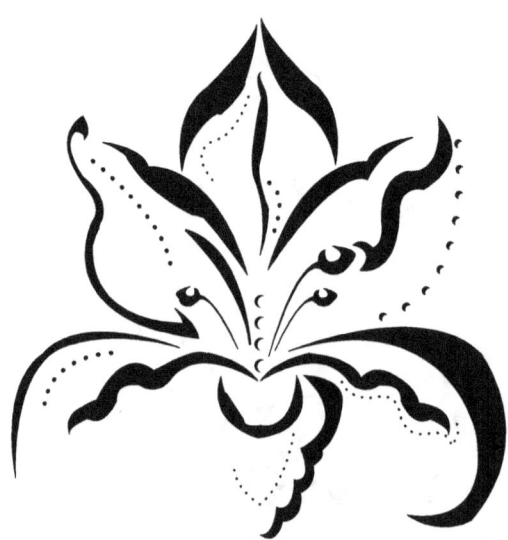

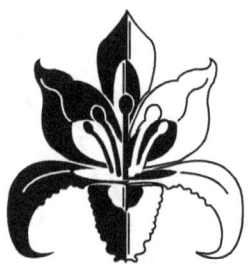

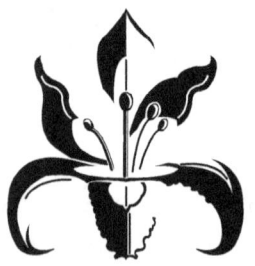

Frog 2
Jeremy Kennedy

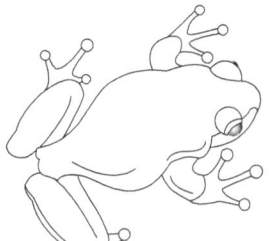

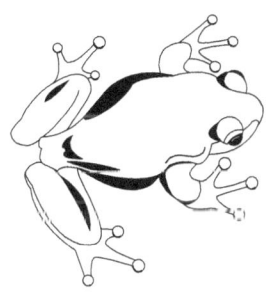

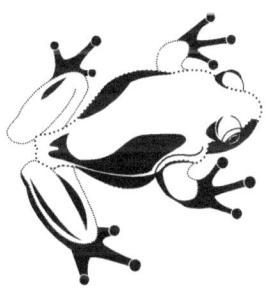

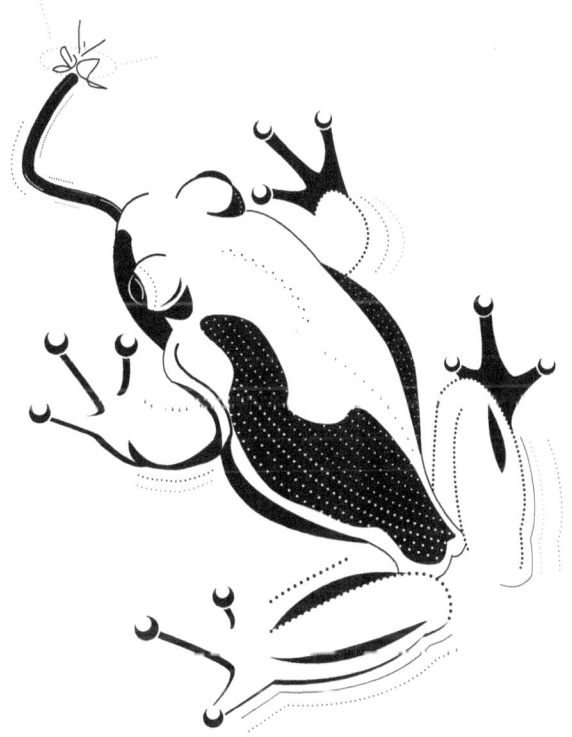

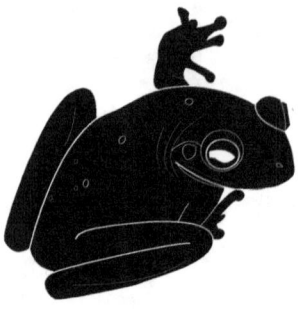

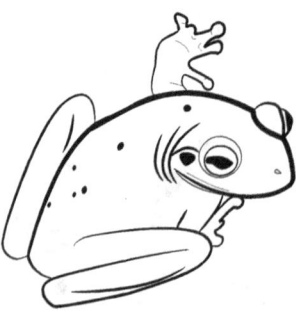

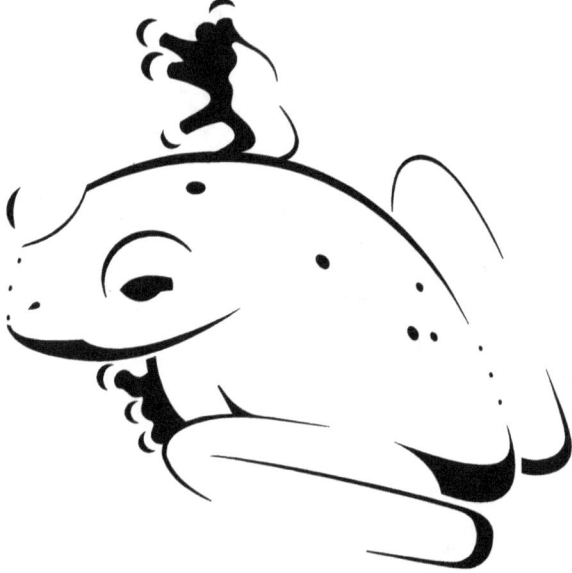

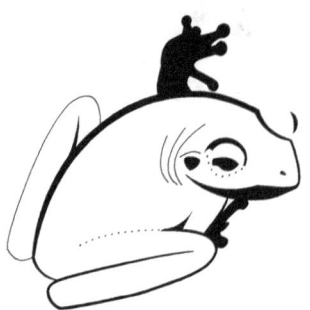

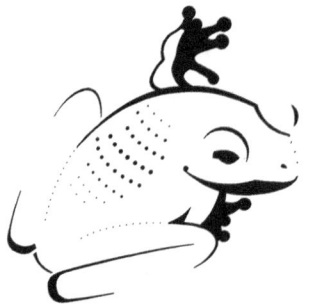

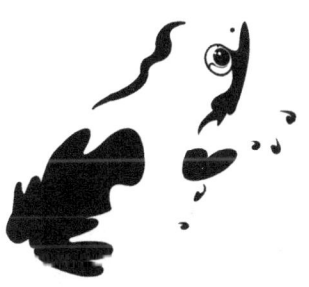

Frog 4
Melody Naylor

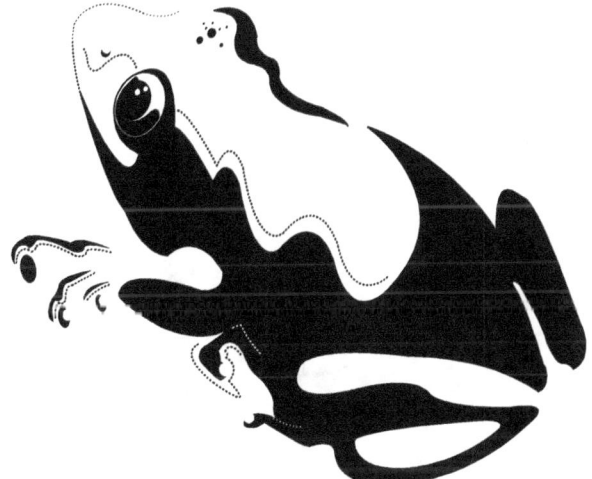

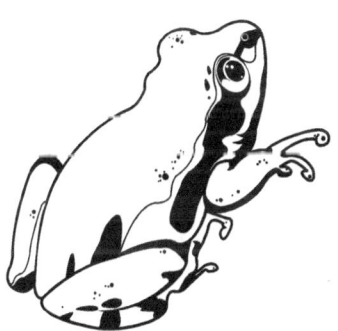

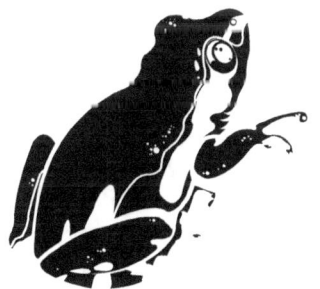

Fish
Jana Dee Bassingthwaite

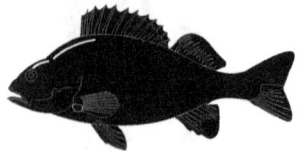

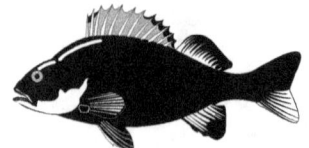
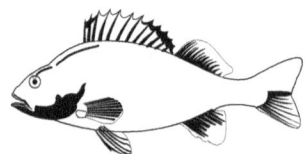
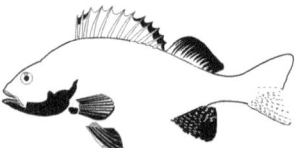

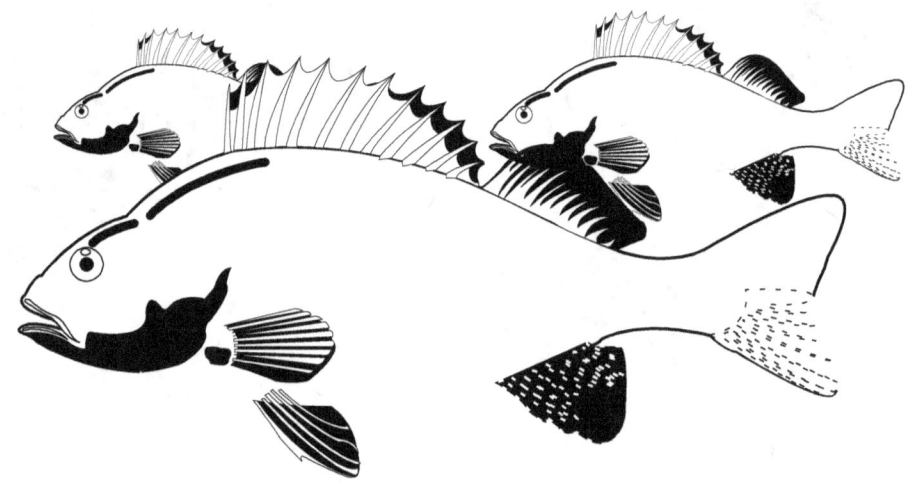

Grasshopper

Drew Tyndell

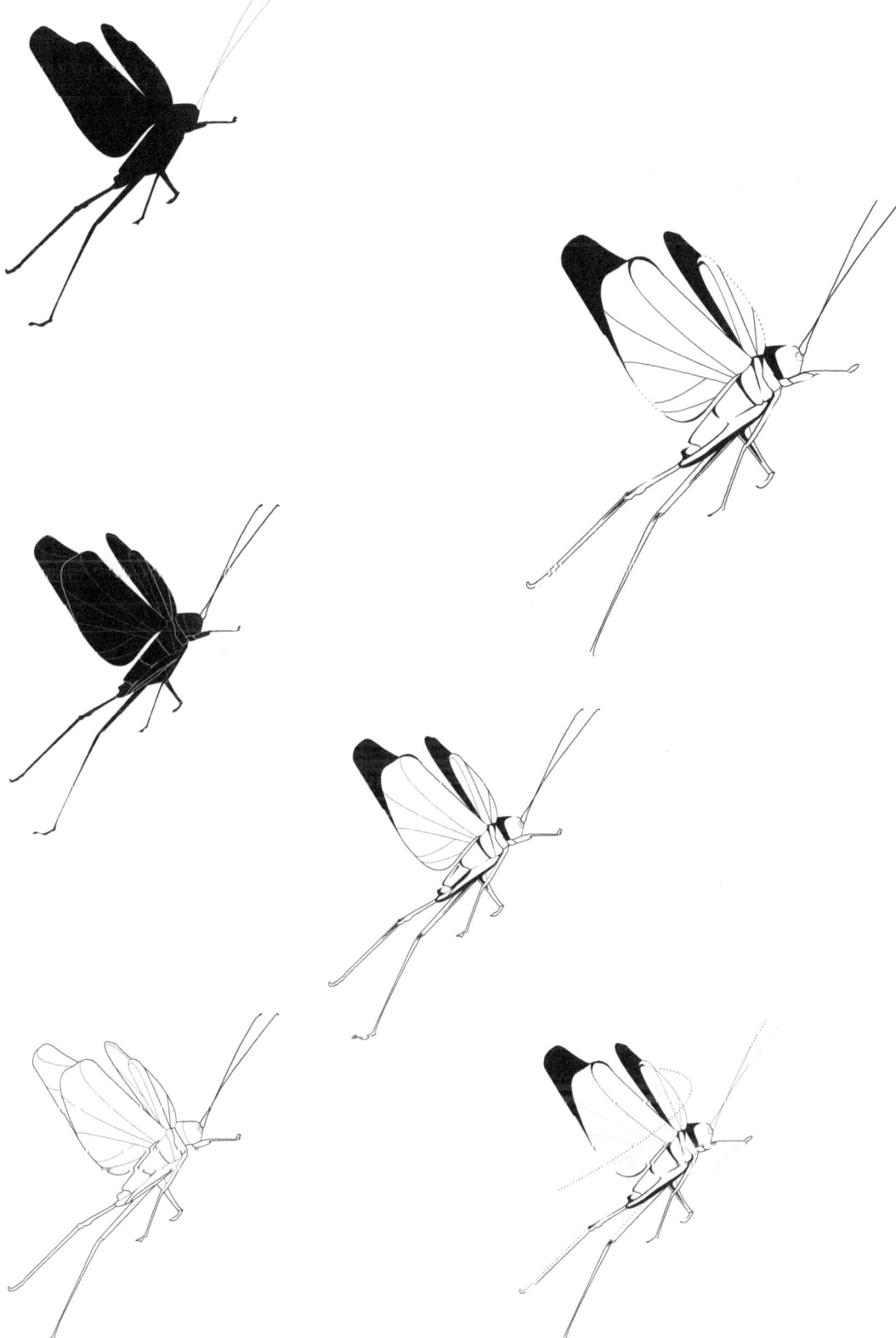

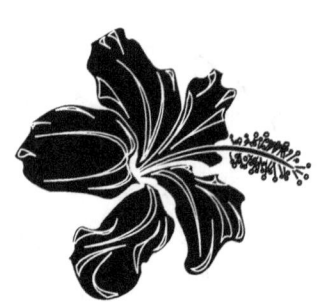

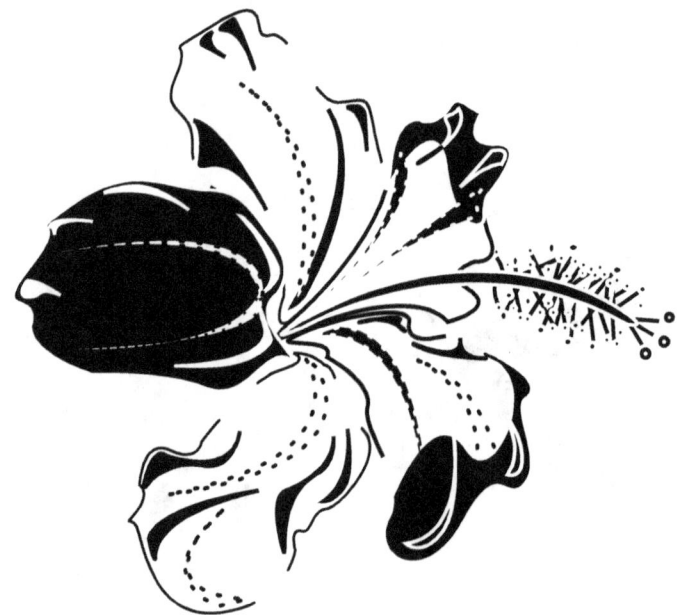

Lizard

Ronnie Koff

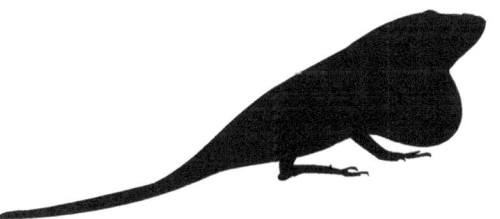

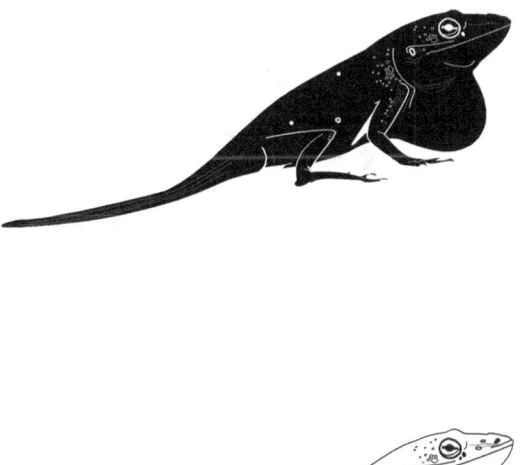

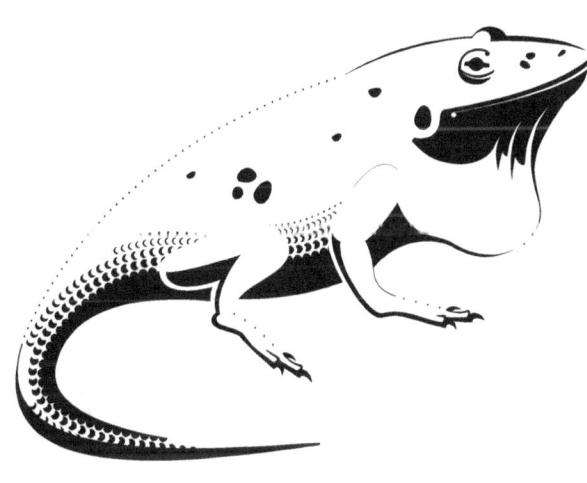

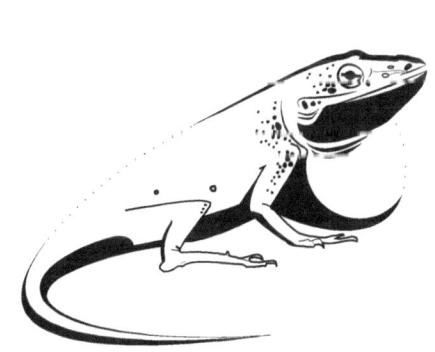

Lady Bug 2

Heather Hickman

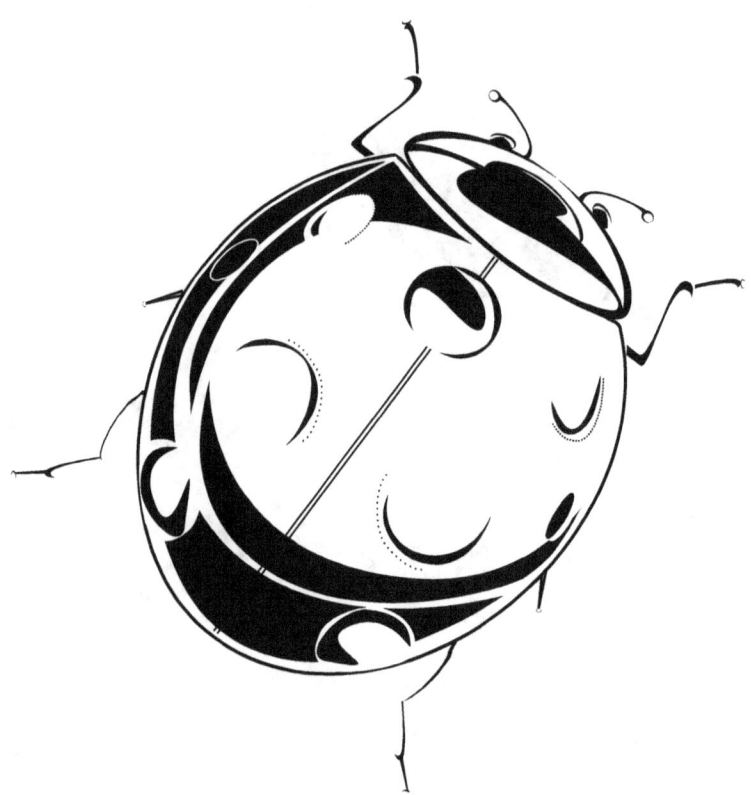

Translation Process
The early versions of the lady bug are static and
fairly predictable. By the third step in the translation the designer began to create highlights
and shadows which make the insect far more
interesting. The final steps in the translation
reveal an ability to develop the drawing with
insight and imagination.

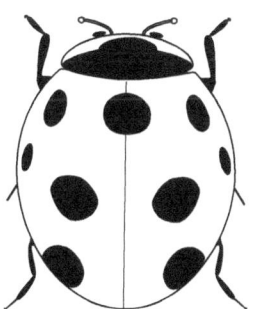

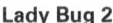

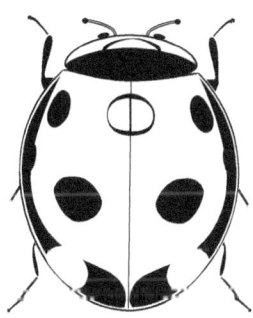

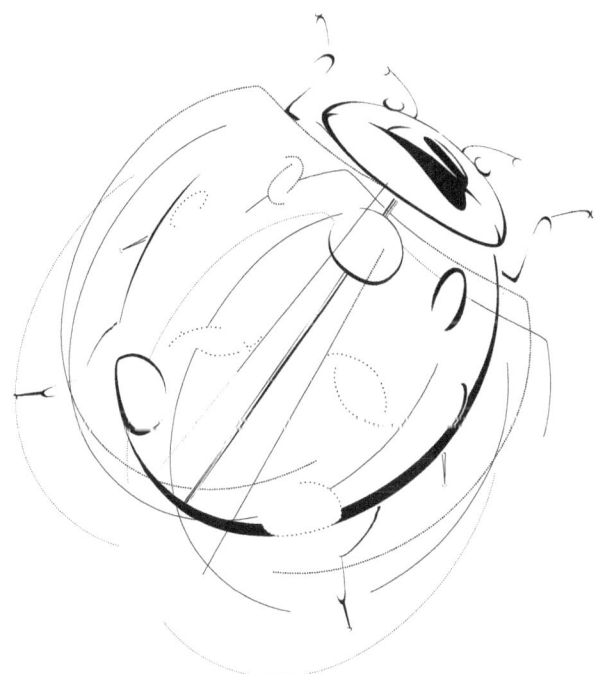

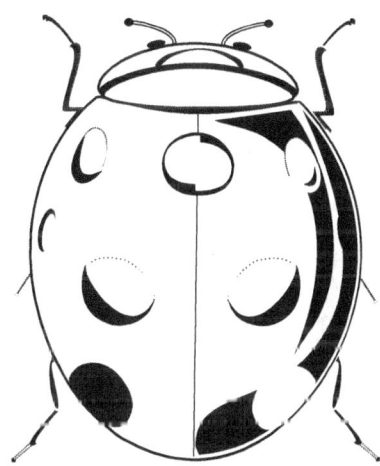

Lobster 1

Keishea Edwards

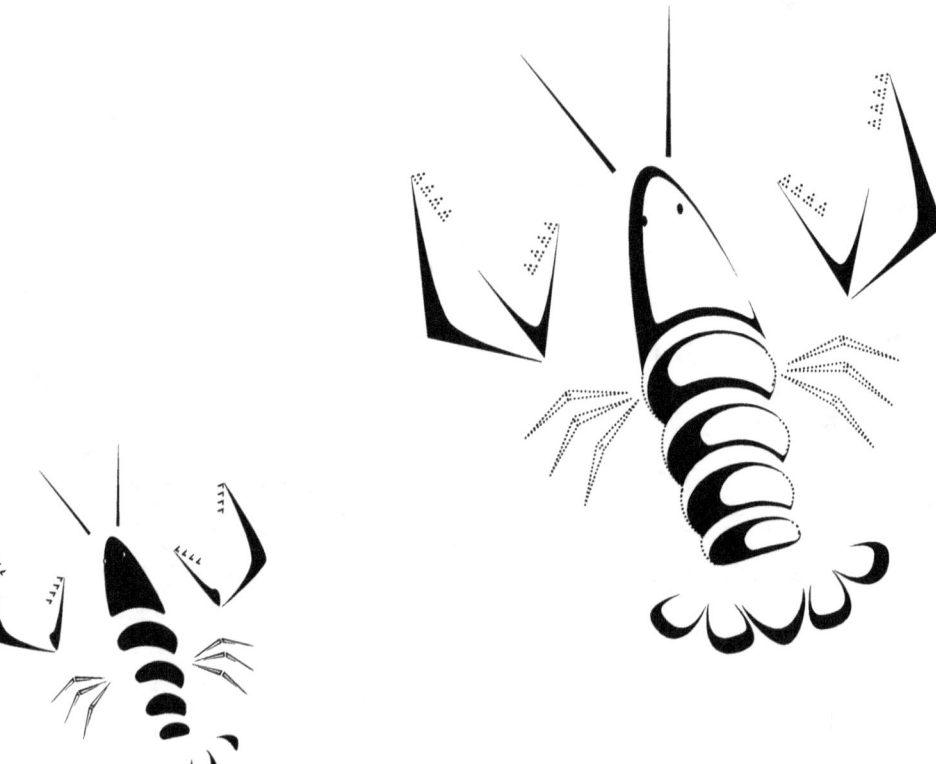

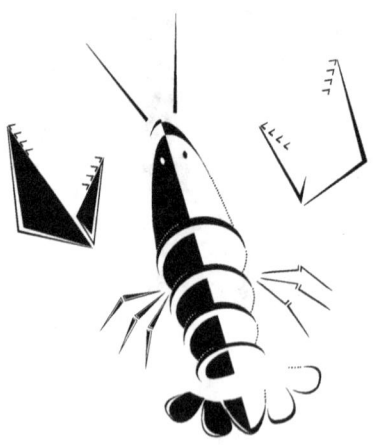

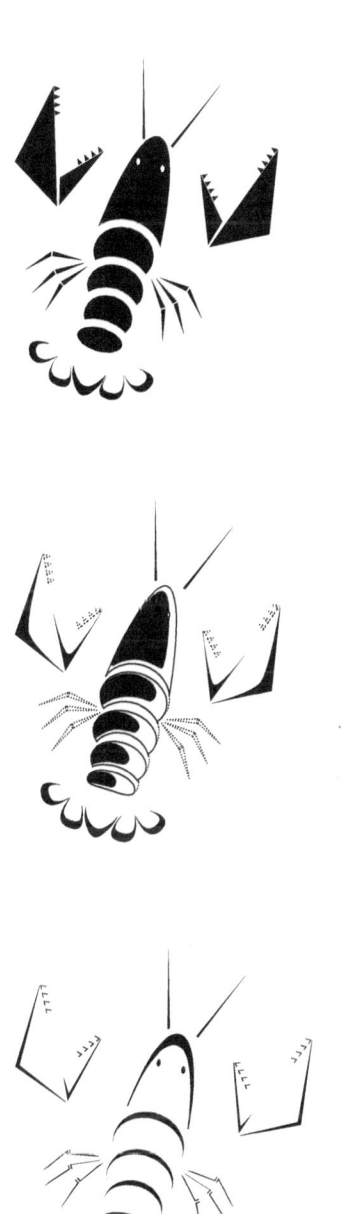

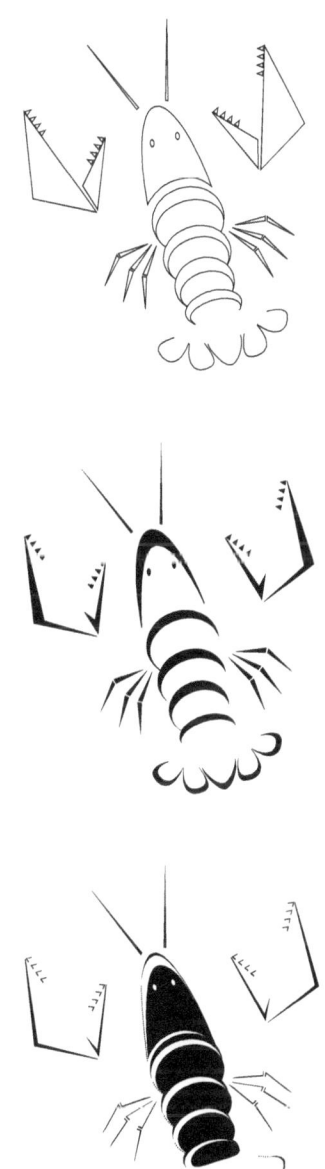

Lobster 2

Jana Dee Bassingthwaite

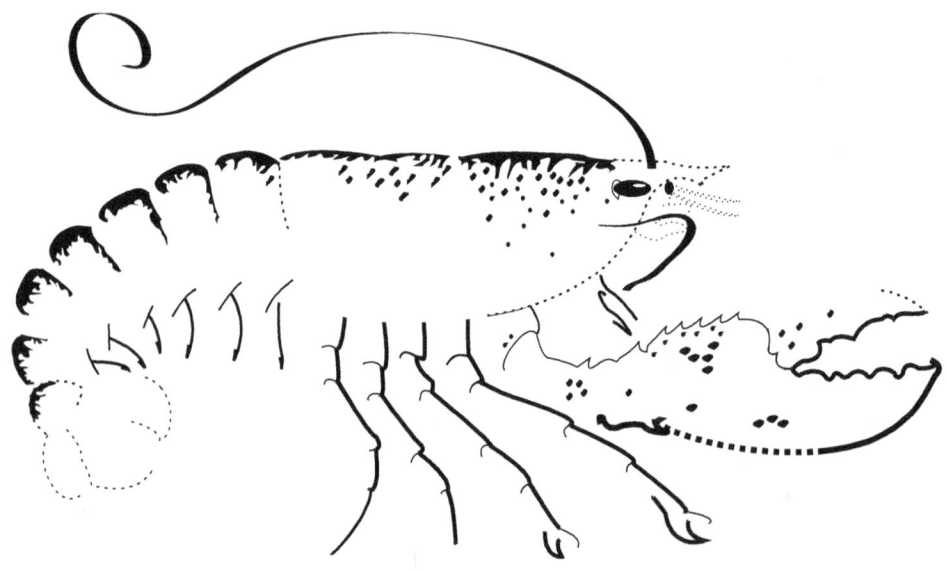

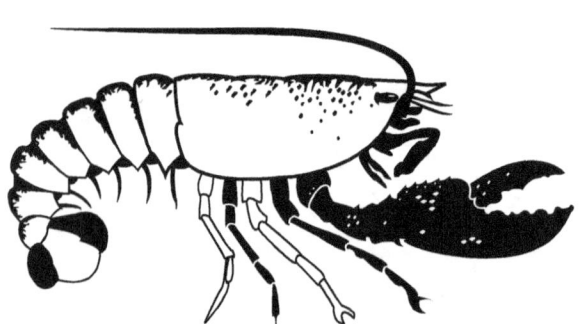

Lobster 2
Jana Dee Bassingthwaite

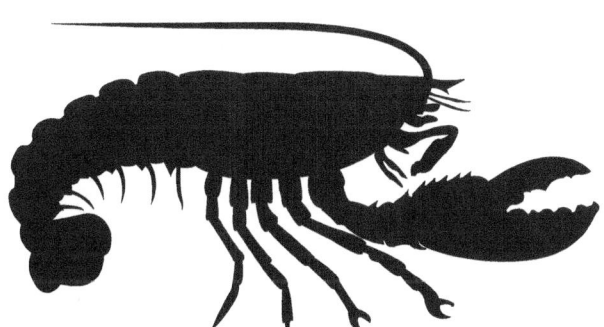

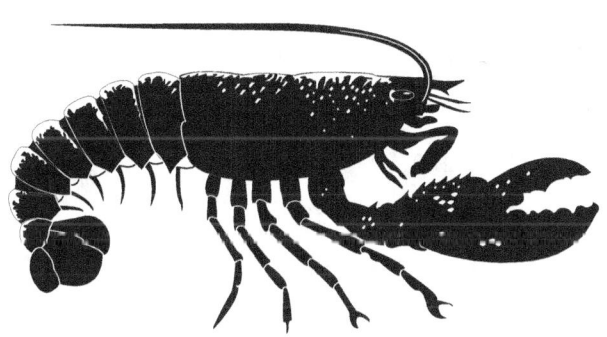

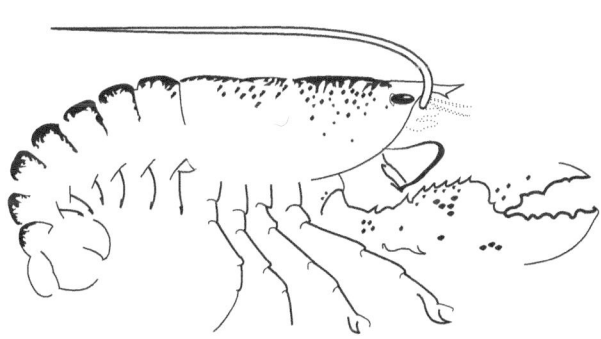

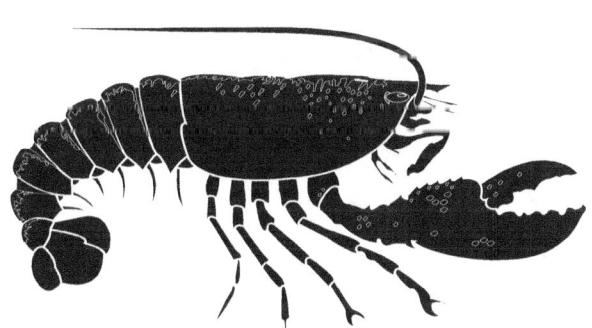

129

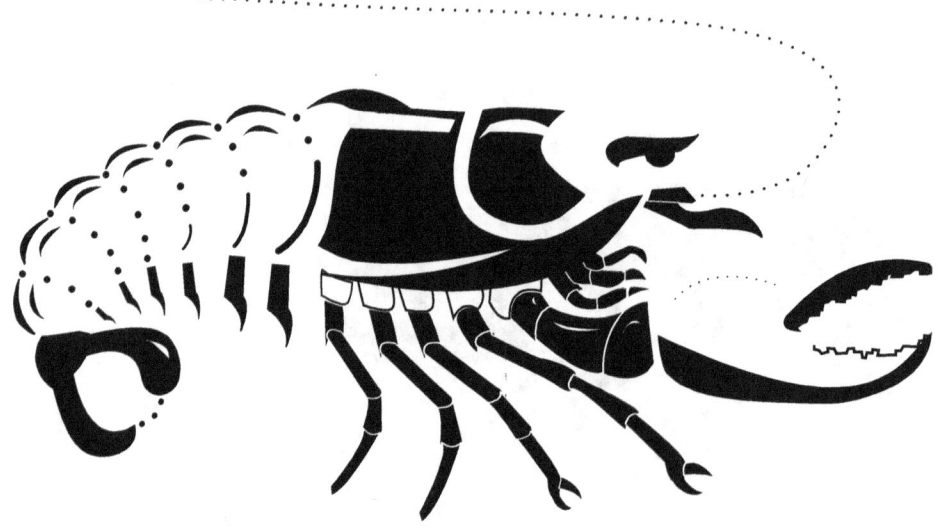

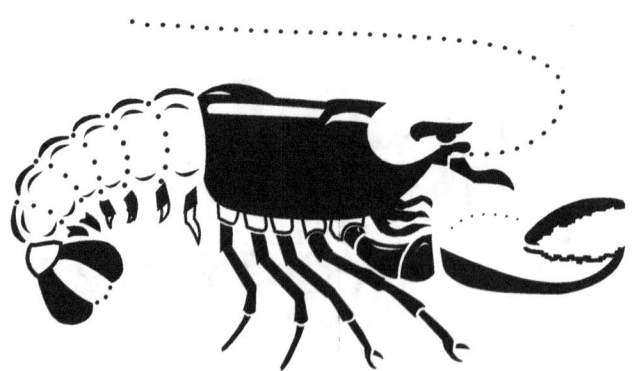

Lobster 3

Annie Riker

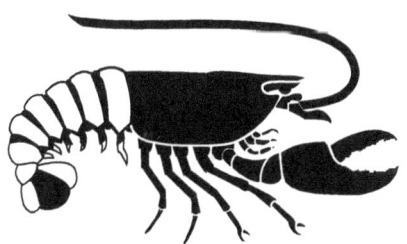

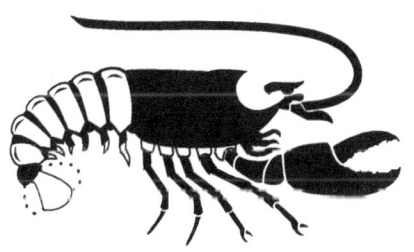

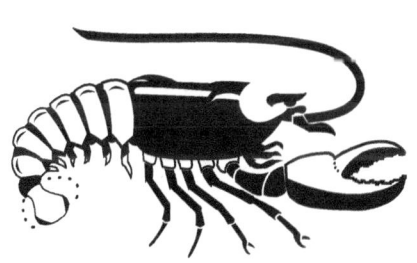

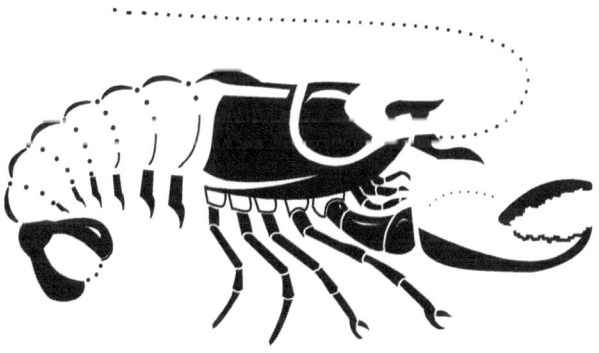

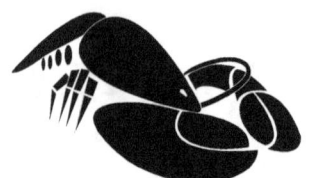

Lobster 4

Geoff Pawlaczyk

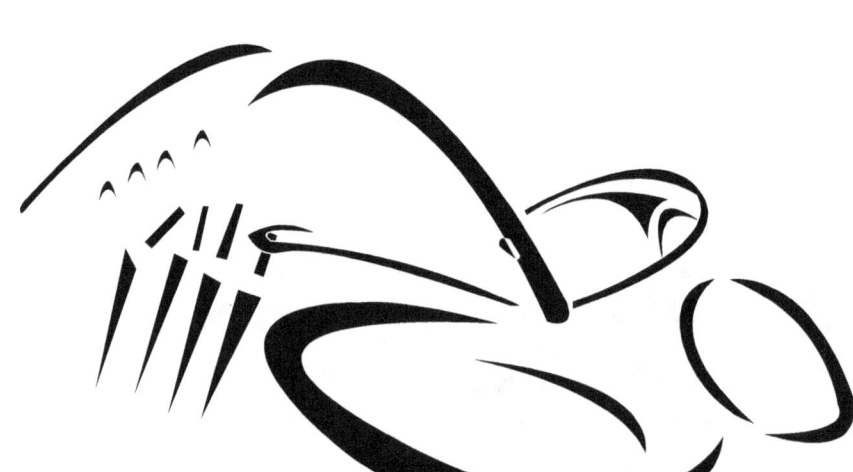

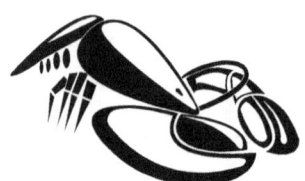

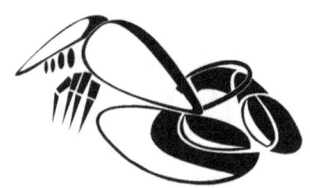

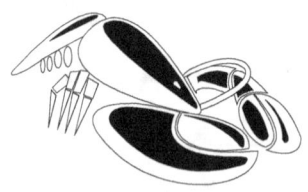

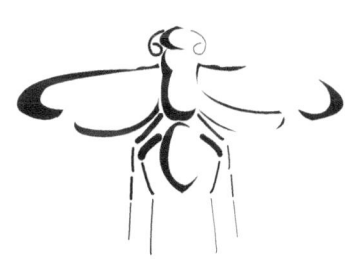

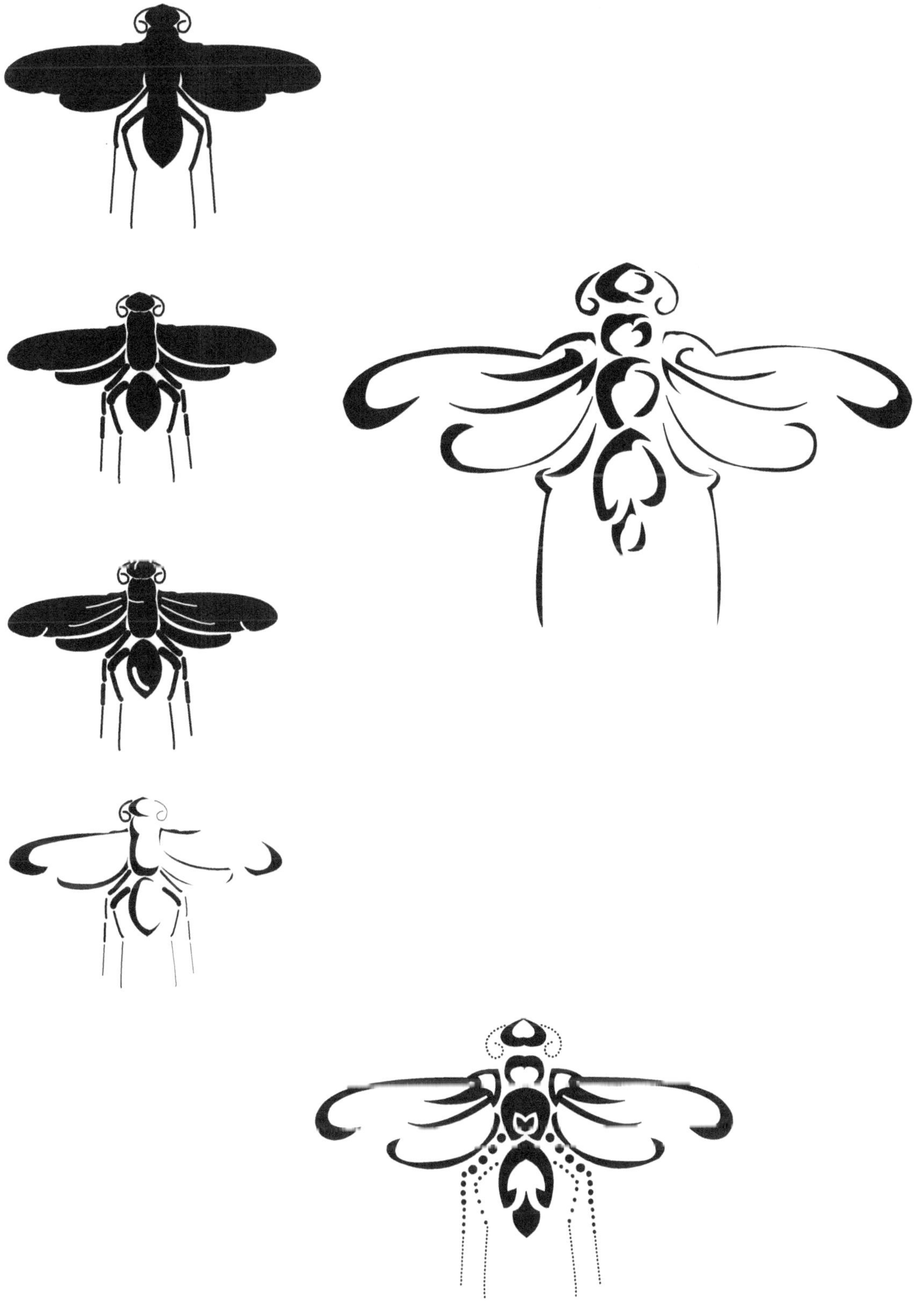

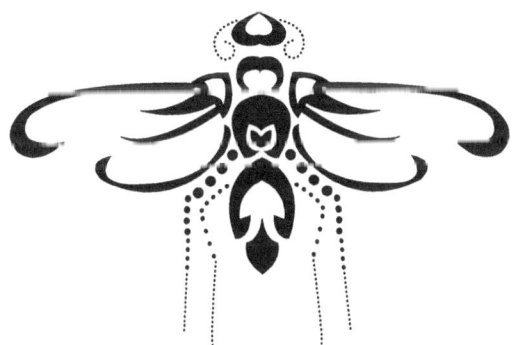

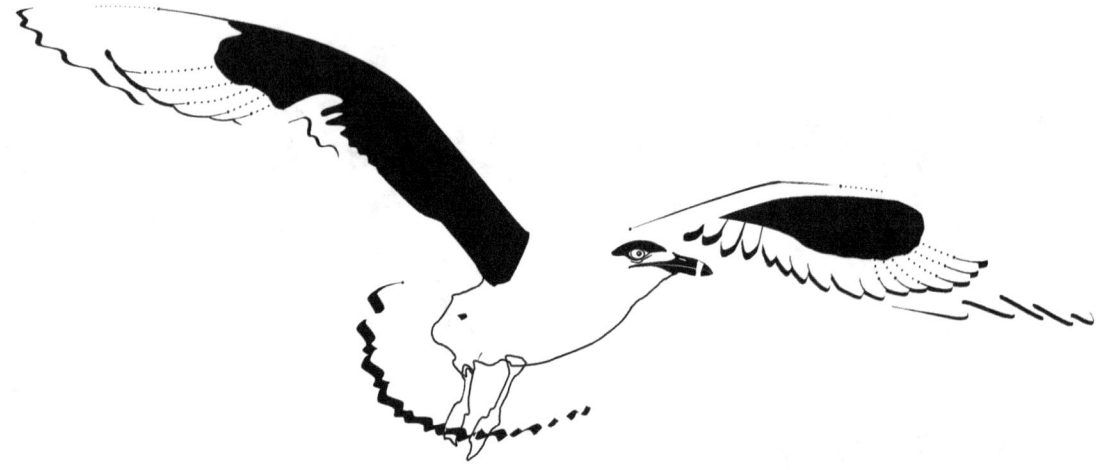

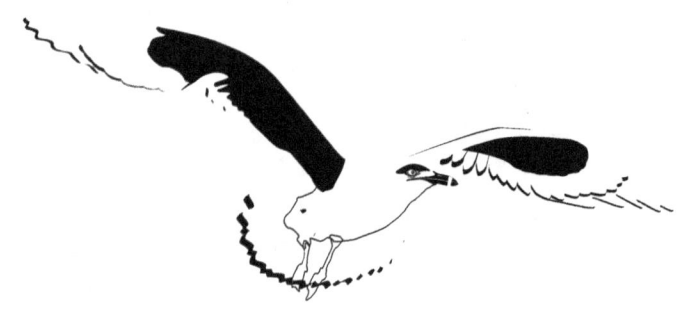

Seagull 2
Tommy Bradley

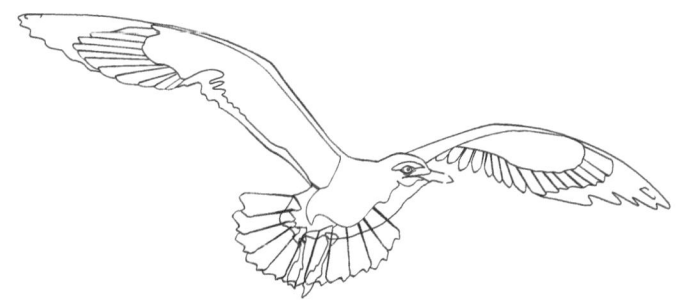

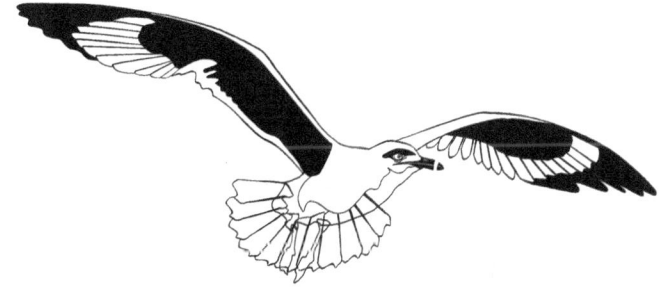

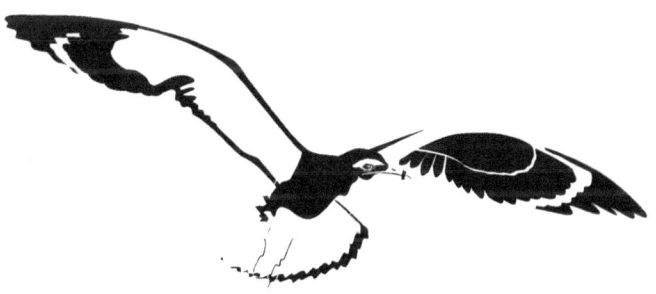

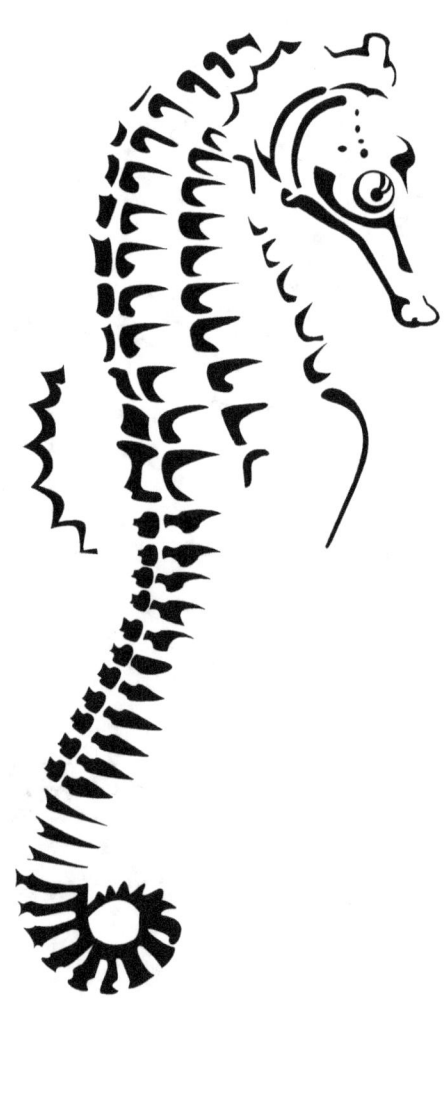

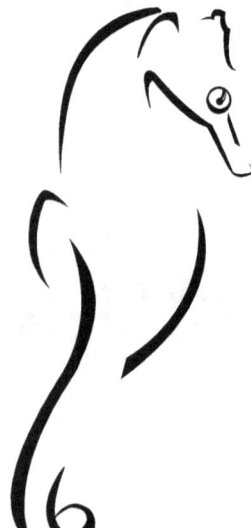

Seahorse
Emily O'Neal

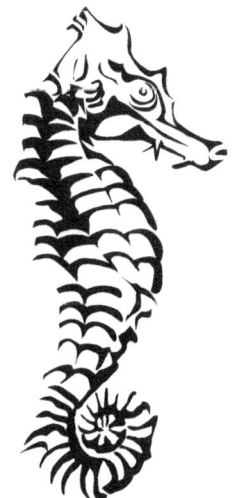

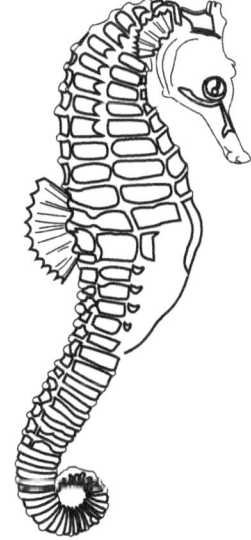

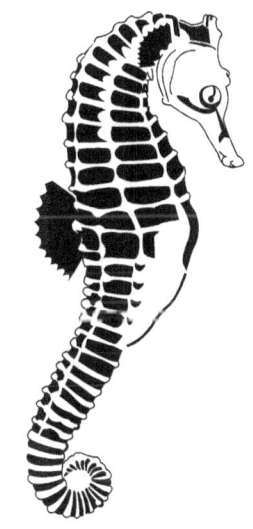

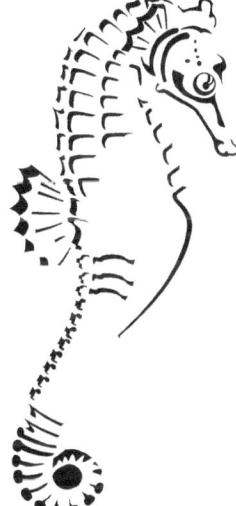

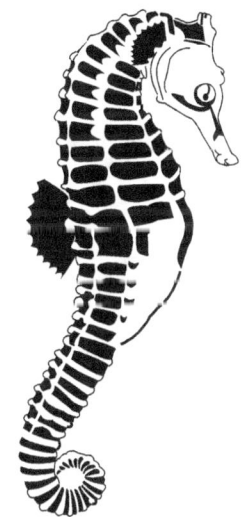

Snail 1
Melissa Pena

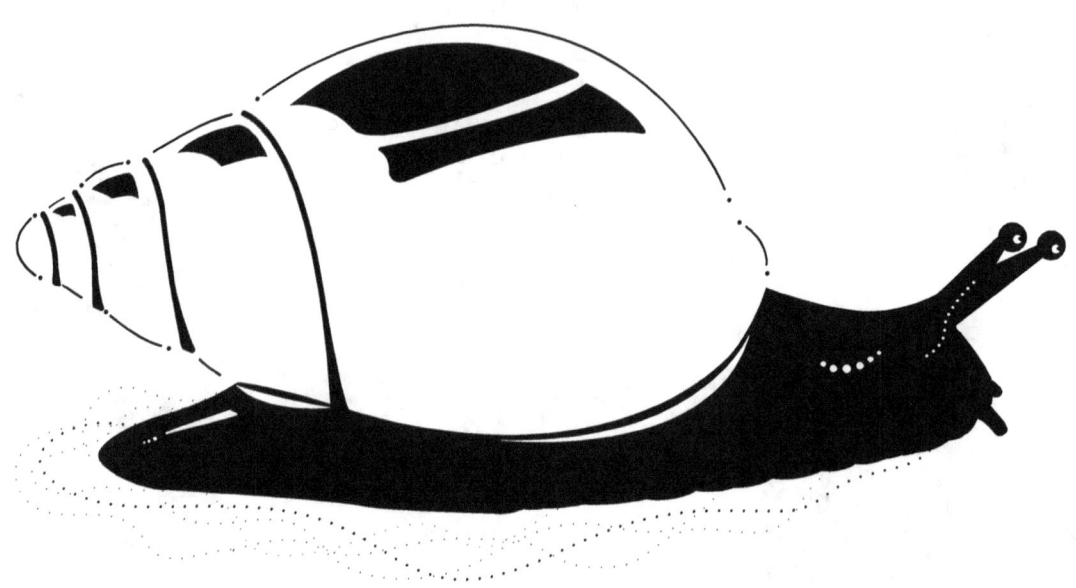

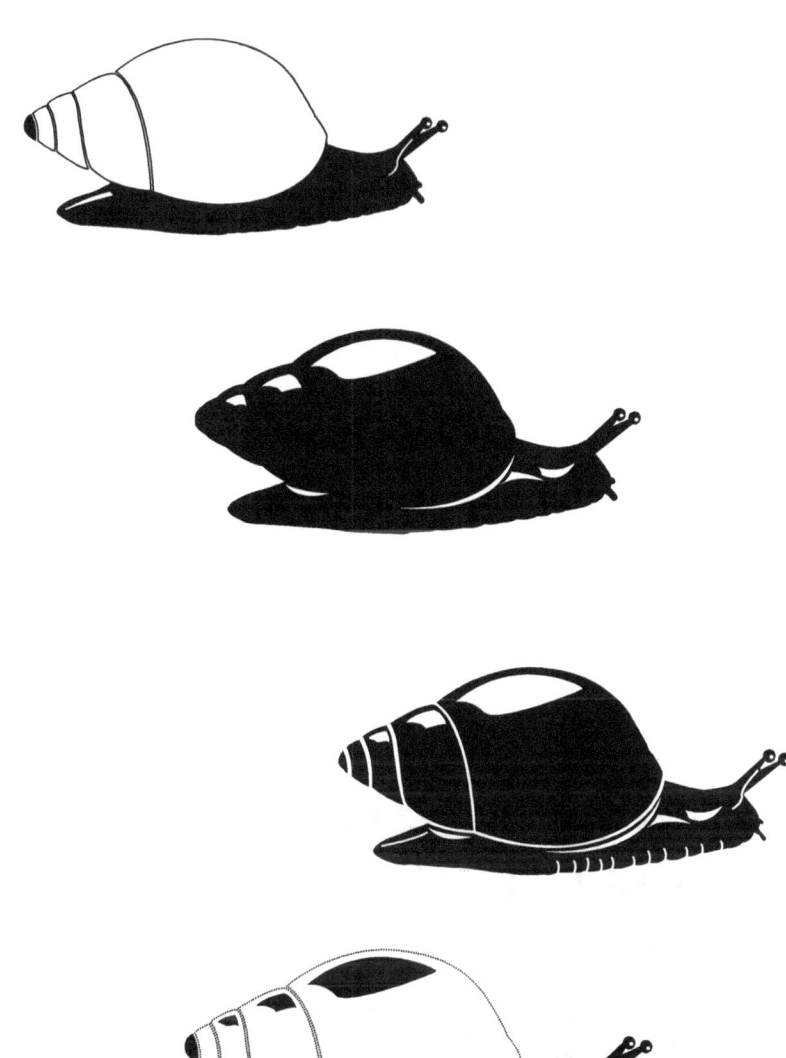

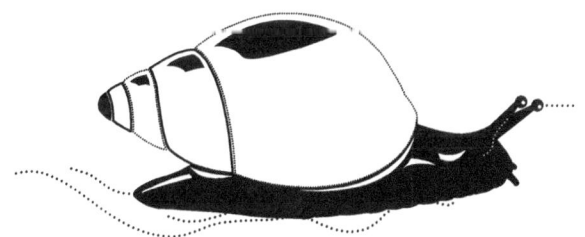

Snail 2

Christopher Roeleveld

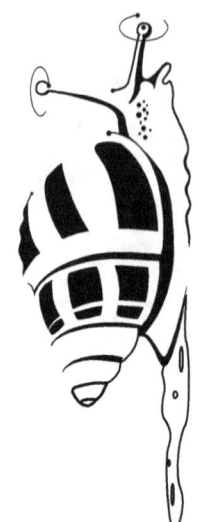

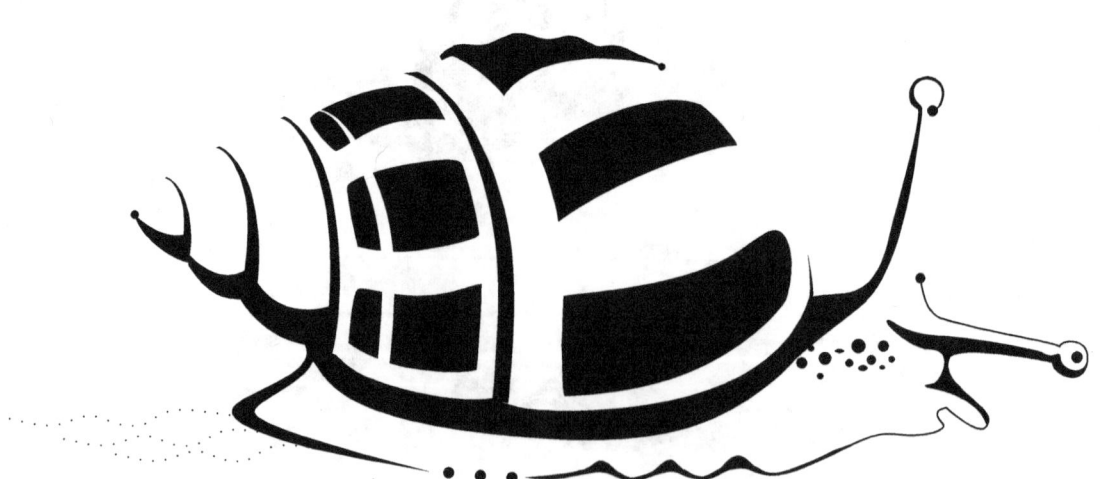

Snail 2
Christopher Roeleveld

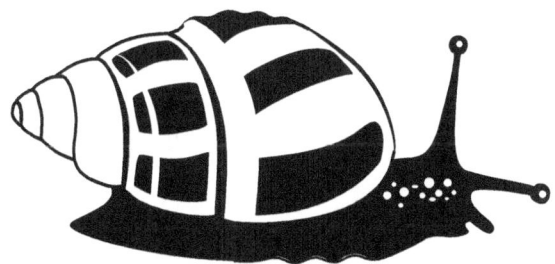

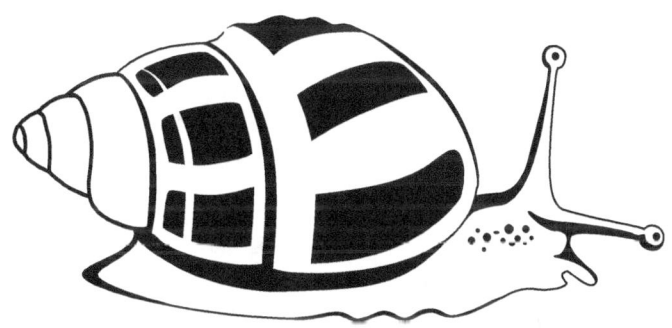

Spider
Jorge Lamora

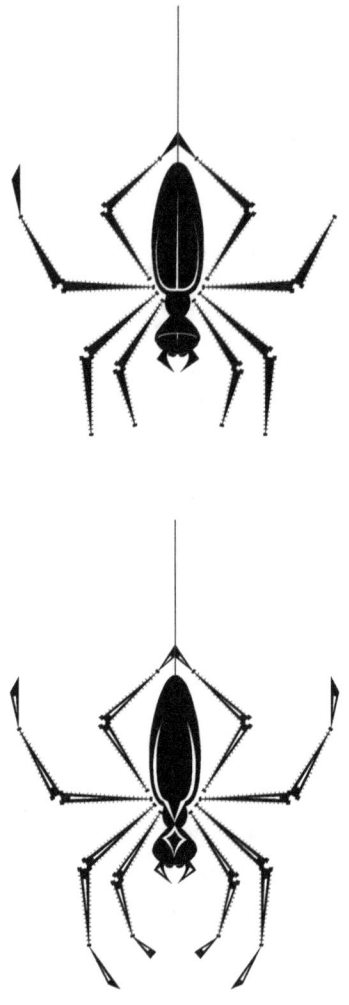

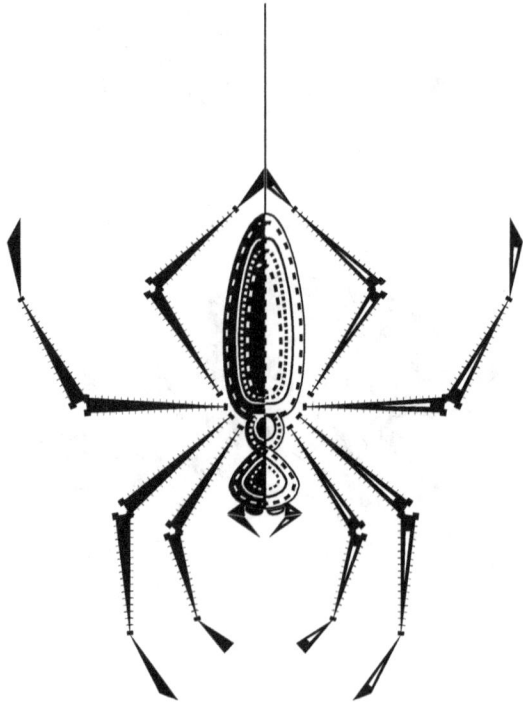

Fine Texture
The fine lines on the legs of the spider are stylized hair that give the spider a texture. This object is also completly symmetrical, and when drawn only one half needs to be drawn and then copied and reflected to complete the object.

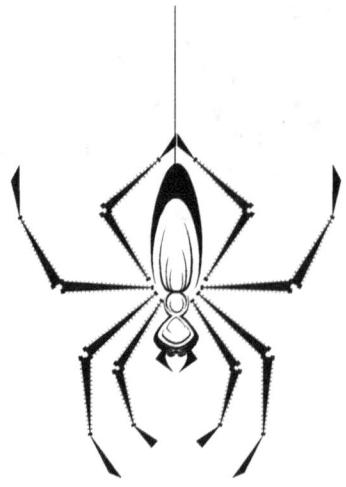

Shark
Geoff Pawlaczyk

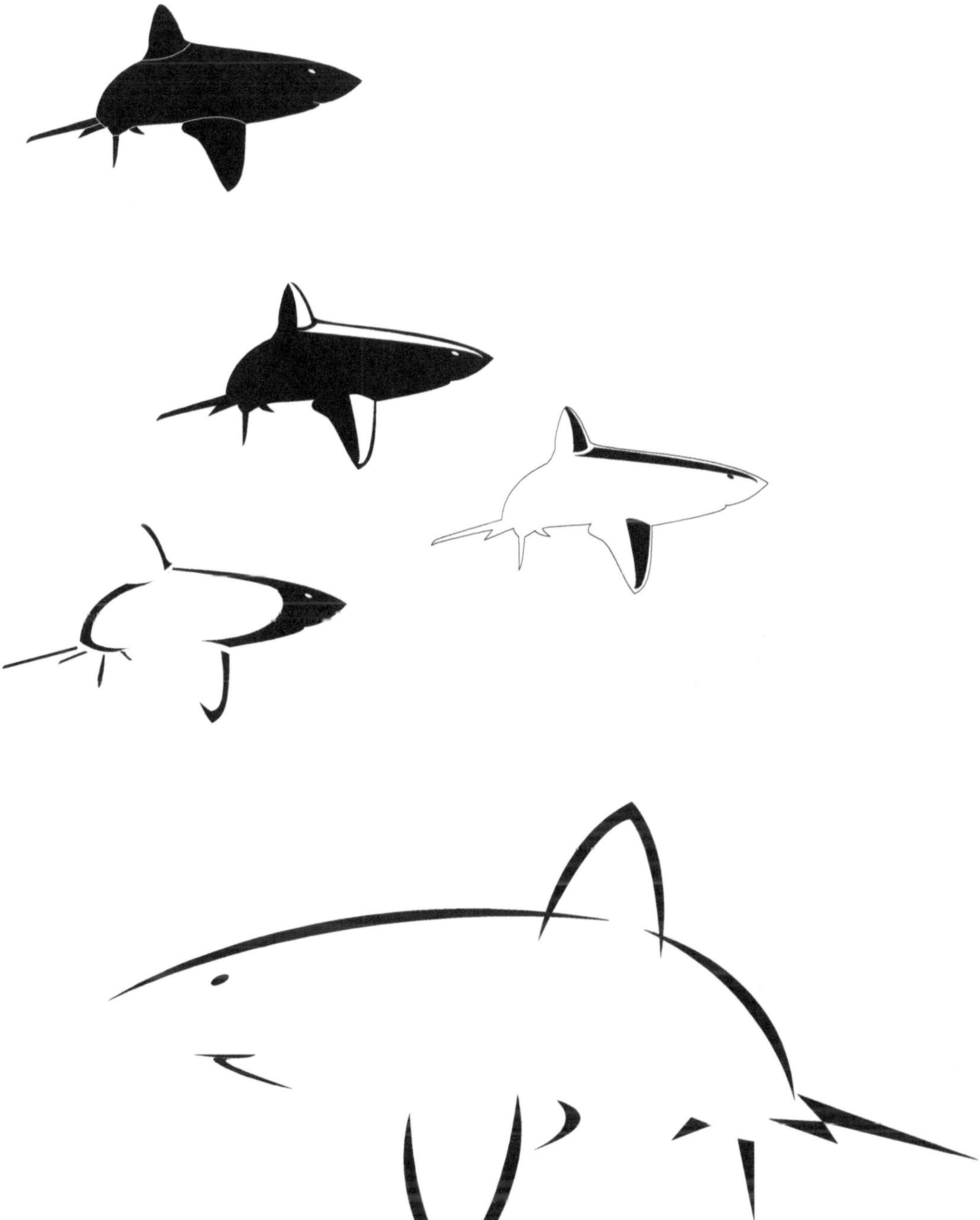

143

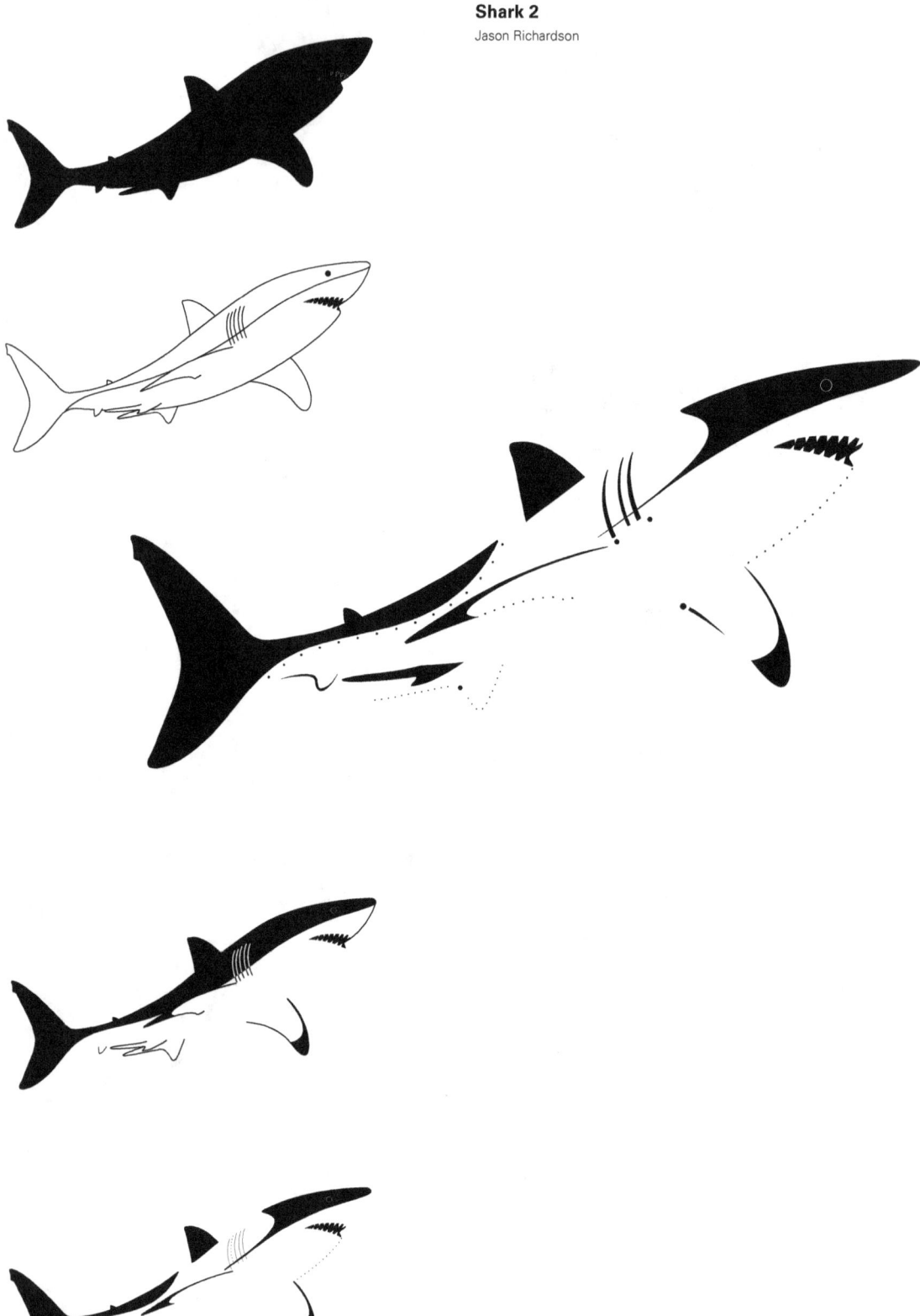

www.ingramcontent.com/pod-product-compliance
Lightning Source LLC
Chambersburg PA
CBHW080413290526
45791CB00008BA/2261